The Insider's Guide to Being a Brilliant Grandparent

Phill Williams

Editor: Roni Jay

new tricks for old dogs

Published by White Ladder Press Ltd

Great Ambrook, Near Ipplepen, Devon T

01803 813343

www.whiteladderpress.com

First published in Great Britain in 2007

10 9 8 7 6 5 4 3 2 1

© Phill Williams 2007

The right of Phill Williams to be identified as author of this work has been asserted by him in accordance with the Copyright, Designs and Patents Act 1988.

ISBN 978 1 905410 17 0

British Library Cataloguing in Publication Data

A CIP record for this book can be obtained from the British Library.

Designed and typeset by Julie Martin Ltd
Cover design by Julie Martin Ltd
Cover photograph Jonathon Bosley

Printed and bound by TJ International Ltd, Padstow, Cornwall
Cover printed by St Austell Printing Company
Printed on totally chlorine-free paper
The paper used for the text pages of this book is FSC certified.
FSC (The Forest Stewardship Council) is an international
network to promote responsible management of the world's forests.

FSC

Mixed Sources

Product group from well-managed forests and other controlled sources

Cert no. SGS-COC-2482
www.fsc.org
© 1996 Forest Stewardship Council

 White Ladder books are distributed in the UK by Virgin Books

White Ladder Press
Great Ambrook, Near Ipplepen, Devon TQ12 5UL
01803 813343
www.whiteladderpress.com

Acknowledgements

I'm grateful to the many grandparents and grandchildren, too many to mention by name, who so willingly contributed so much of the material gathered for this book. Particular thanks are due to my local primary school and WI for helping in the venture.

Some of the humorous stories about grandparents and grandchildren appeared on the **www.butler** website on the internet, and I thank the unknown individuals who put them there. The site of the Grandparents Association, **www.grandparents-association.org.uk** was a source of direct help over difficult issues, and is well worth consulting. Two other sources deserving a mention for their comments on specific situations are Virginia Spurlock's delightful and amusing book 'Have Grandchildren, will Travel' and Neil Ferguson's more serious 'Grandparenting in Divorced Families'.

Several individuals read the various drafts. I particularly value the constructive, detailed and tactful suggestions made by my editors at White Ladder, Roni and Rich. JB offered helpful comments and RH not only read and commented, but also provided love, support and encouragement throughout the whole enterprise. I'm also greatly indebted to Irma Kurtz for her willingness to contribute the endorsement that appears on the cover.

Lastly, but most importantly, my three children, Gareth, Gwyneth, Peter, and their spouses have produced seven children – Bronwen, Patrick, Harry, Rory, Ian, Owen and Jonathon. They have unwittingly provided the experiences that have spurred me to write the book: thanks to all of you – without you there certainly wouldn't have been a book at all!

Contents

Introduction

"Grandparents are a lady and a man who have no little children of their own. They like other people's."

Are there a lot of grandparents about? Probably more than most people realise; over 13 million in 2005. More than three-quarters of us become grandparents at some point in our lives, which means that most of us will have to learn about a new relationship, a relationship with grandchildren. Learn, I hear some of you ask? Surely we don't have to learn about being grandparents? We've brought up children, we've been there before. You can't teach your *grandmother,* of all people, to suck eggs.

Well, that view probably explains why there are so few books on grandparenting. Search the shelves of your local bookshop and you'll probably find a good selection of books on bringing up children, but you'll be lucky to find more than one or two on grandparenting. Trawl the internet, and you'll find a few specialised books, largely American. But as the next chapter indicates, grandparents are changing, attitudes to grandparents are changing, and our place in a changing society is more important than it used to be. One obvious example is the vastly increased number of working mothers with young children, and the greater call on grandparents for help. This is in tension with the much greater scattering of families today. Many grandparents no longer live 'just around the corner', and can't help with the children as their own parents did. These and other changes mean that it's a good moment to look again at those many situations that give pleasure to grandparents, those that require some skill, and to find out how modern grandparents handle both.

One or two courses on grandparenting have appeared, but don't worry: this book isn't going to try to teach. Rather, it's intended to offer some information on the pleasures to be enjoyed and the pitfalls to be avoided. And it's not dogma presented from some expert, but largely the views and experiences of the real experts, those modern grandmothers and grandfathers who took the trouble to fill in our questionnaire, as well as those whom we talked to informally, making over 100 responders in all. Many of them also wrote about their experiences and discussed these with us. And be warned: we also interviewed some 50 grandchildren, who wrote about and talked about their experiences with their grandparents. So the book includes a small selection of 'consumer' opinions too.

Any book is bound to be based to some extent on the life of the author, and this book is no exception. As the father of three children, and grandfather of seven grandchildren, four of whom live overseas, I've also drawn on my own experiences of grandparenting. Some of these experiences appear as personal comments, while others (perhaps fortunately) will be recognised only by my family.

The book itself is divided into different chapters, or themes, but of course there's no need to read them in sequence: any one can be dipped into when needed. To put matters in a nutshell, the relationship with your grandchildren can be a wonderfully happy one, and a little forethought helps to ensure that it will be. And happy grandparenting!

CHAPTER 1

Little Beginnings and Big Moments

"When your new little grandchild holds your little finger in his little fist, you're hooked for life."

Hearing the News

So you've had that phone call at last. They've rung with the glad tidings, and you're really going to be a grandparent. You've been waiting – how many years? – and you've been so good about it, so patient. You haven't dropped any hints, haven't said how pleased your friends are with their new grandchild, haven't wondered pointedly what they're doing about it, or complained to your friends about how slow they are.

Now those pleasant images of little darlings running around once more, asking to be cuddled, or wanting to be thrown up in the air and caught, those images will be real. That wonderfully infectious childhood laughter will ring round the house again. You can muse wistfully over those happy shots of your own children when they were little, dust down those old toys up in the attic, bring out those old books you used to read to them. You can – must – tell all your friends, break the good news over a coffee, perhaps hold a little party. Hey, it's exciting! Many many congratulations!

Rethink

But wait a minute. Just pause: let a tiny glimpse of the other side cast the tiniest of shadows on this idyllic picture of yours. Have another look at those old photographs. That happy shot of little

Jack playing on the beach – wasn't that when he dropped his ice cream in the sand, threw that terrific temper tantrum and couldn't or wouldn't be comforted? It spoiled everybody's day out: remember that? And that shot of little Sophie, hand in hand with you, going off to the shops – wasn't that the day you turned round to find her having a call of nature in the middle of one of the supermarket aisles? Think how embarrassed you were by the black looks of those fastidious assistants who came to clean it up.

Yes, having little children in the family again isn't all sweetness and light. But of course, this will be different. They won't be your children: you'll be a grandparent – the parents have all the responsibilities and you have the enjoyment. Hm: not entirely true. After all, Jack and Sophie could well have been with their grandparents when those situations blew up.

There are a few grandparents-to-be who may be apprehensive, and worry about the effect that a grandchild may have on their lives. Pause for a moment and remember the statistic quoted in the Introduction: more than three-quarters of us become grandparents at some time in our lives. So most of us have stood where you are standing now. And most of us grandparents feel that the presence of a new arrival in the family, the changing relationships with our children, the whole new set of experiences that a grandchild brings, all of this has enriched our lives immeasurably.

When a grandchild is born, we enter a new relationship with a new little person. It will have its moments, like all relationships. So we can't expect a wonderful, beautiful fairy story all the time. But if we're prepared to brush up those old qualities we honed on our own children, the patience, ingenuity, tolerance and so on... and top them all with the lashings of love we feel, the awkward moments will be very few and far between.

Help!

Yes, they really have rung: pregnant at last. The first glow of pleasure floods through you. Your own child is starting a family, just like you did all those years ago. The words, the warm response, jump to your lips before you even think about them.

"What wonderful news!"

What did you think of when you heard the news? Did your thoughts flash back to when you first started a family? Or was your first thought one of doting grandparents playing with happy babies? Or of enjoying family Christmases with children again? Or did you have at the same time a slight sinking feeling, as you began to wonder how your children would cope? Times are different now, and both parents are probably leading busy working lives. Will both new parents want to follow the modern trend, and get back to their jobs as soon as possible? You remember well the demands and responsibilities of bringing up children, how they filled your life. How will the new parents be able to fit these in with the demands of their work?

Delight and slight apprehension are both entirely natural reactions. And you wouldn't be human if you didn't wonder what the news meant for your life, too. But you're a generous person, and the words flow out:

"Oh we'll help you, we really will!"

Let's think of your offer to help. Help with caring for the baby? Help in the house? Help financially? Help.... What exactly did you mean, and more importantly, what did the offer of help mean to the parents?

Early Interference

First, is an offer of help what the parent-to-be wants to hear?

Probably. Yet it's worth remembering that some young couples have this happy illusion that they don't need any help. You know the sort of thing; 'Oh we're not going to let the baby change our lives at all', said with the confidence of youth. They'll learn, you say to yourself, as you bite your tongue and smile at them. I recall the couple I met feeding their six month old baby half way up Cradle Mountain, New Zealand, in a heatwave. The baby wasn't going to make them change their backpacking holidays: no way. Admiration for their independence was mixed with worry about the effect of the hot sun on the baby, who next day was quite dangerously ill.

But there are some parents-to-be who are not just proudly independent, but genuinely suspicious of help, fearing it might turn into the dreaded interference from the grandparents. They may want to bring up their baby in their way, a different way, a modern way, uncontaminated by what they see as old-fashioned routines and ideas. So tread carefully before offering unconditional assistance.

And you'll be far too wise to try to force help on the new family. I recall the story of the grandparent who was so determined that *her* grandchild wasn't going to be placed in a creche, that she insisted on coming to stay and look after the baby while the parents worked. What a wonderful offer, the parents thought at first. Before too long, grandma gradually began to run the household, they felt their lives were not their own, and the inevitable explosion occurred.

Early Commitments

And what if the parents-to-be are sensible, and want to use any offers of help that fit their needs? It's worth wondering what they imagine your offer means. Does it conjure up thoughts of grandparents paying for little Joseph's education? Or 'grandma's' as a place where a child can be left every day while mother carries on with her career as before? Or of grandpa always being around to meet the youngster from school, a lesser duty perhaps, but an obligation nevertheless? The parents-to-be may not yet have thought through the sort of help they'll need. (We touch on some of these issues in Chapter 7.) But now, right at the beginning, you might want to think carefully about the kind of help that you both want to give and are able to give.

So at the right moment, it's important to talk about help, rather than offering a fully comprehensive insurance policy immediately. Perhaps 'accidents and emergencies only' might be a more suitable arrangement for some grandparents. Or some sort of intermediate arrangement might fit some situations better. 'Negotiations' sounds an unfeeling word to use for the start of a wonderful new relationship, but it's usually wiser to talk sooner about how much help you might be able to give, rather than having to disappoint later.

Exciting times; times when the relationship with your children begins to change. Yes, they're still your children, but they've matured: they're about to become parents too. They're also going to become experts in child-rearing, and so they may begin to treat you on equal terms, as fellow adults. Enjoy it!

So, to summarise:

- The news of a grandchild-to-be is one of life's very exciting moments: enjoy it, share it with your friends!

- Prepare now for a life enriching set of experiences. Talk to other grandparents about the changes in their lives. Read some of the books mentioned in the Acknowledgements. Make a note of the Grandparents Association (also in Acknowledgements) for future reference.

- Don't get carried away: remember little children aren't always angelic.

● Don't add an open ended offer of help to your expressions of delight.
  – not every family will want it.
  – some may misinterpret it.

● Do think carefully about what you can and want to do to assist.

● And then choose an appropriate moment to discuss this with the parents-to-be.

CHAPTER 2

Grandparents are Changing

"A grandfather is a man grandmother"

The 'Problem Grandparent'

Did you know that in the 1930s and 1940s grandparents were often seen as a bad influence on children's development? For much of the first half of the last century, grandparents were the strict members of an older generation, the disciplinarians in the family, taking the young to task. 'Little children are to be seen and not heard' was the Victorian view still held by many grandparents then. One real life example is the grandmother who, in the 1930s, wouldn't let her granddaughter even clean her shoes on a Sunday, let alone play any games:

"You must learn to keep the Lord's Day."

When more lenient attitudes towards children's behaviour became fashionable, strict grandparents, like the one mentioned above, were seen as problems in child-rearing. Many grandparents found it hard to see their tried and trusted beliefs on bringing up children thrown overboard in favour of the more relaxed views coming into fashion, and some could not resist the temptation to interfere. So the 'problem grandparent' became a well known character. That's a description largely hard to credit nowadays, when child-rearing has changed, and with the change, so attitudes towards grandparents have altered too. Society has evolved, and the roles that grandparents play in the family are now quite different.

The New Fit Grandparent

The great improvement in health is one of the more interesting changes to affect both the place of the grandparents in the family, and the attitudes of the family towards us grandparents. In times past, many grandparents were old and unwell. Life expectancy a century ago was about 20 years less than it is today, so far fewer people survived as fit and well 50 and 60 year olds, able to play an active part in their grandchildren's lives. Remember little Red Riding Hood's grandmother, tucked up in bed, wearing her nightcap, not a support for the little girl, but more of a responsibility for her. Many grandparents were indeed infirm and elderly. (And to replace Grandma with a fierce wolf – that's not too far from how many grandmothers figured in little children's imagination then.)

One set of my own grandparents had died before I was born. I saw quite a lot of the other set, until my grandfather died when I was eight. My grandmother, who lived on, was a formidable old lady, who ruled her family with a rod of iron. So much were her children in fear of her that one of her daughters, knowing how much the old matriarch disapproved of the relationship she had formed, married her lover in secret. For two years she continued to live at home, meeting her husband at weekends, until at last she plucked up enough courage to tell grandmother, when all hell broke loose.

One of my earliest memories is visiting my grandmother's house. Above the black, cast iron fireplace in the living room there hung a print. It showed a white haired old couple sitting on a wooden bench, while at their feet played a couple of young children, both dressed in those white dresses that Victorians used for little boys and girls alike. Under the picture was the text: "Children's children are the crown of old age." The word 'crown' puzzled me. I knew what a crown was: kings and queens wore crowns. How could children be a crown? It must be wrong, I thought.

Now I know that the picture carried two messages. The intended one, that grandchildren crown life's journey, is very true. The unintended one, the idea that grandchildren arrive in old age, was undoubtedly true when the picture was painted. But today, that message has been overtaken by events. Today's grandparents don't sit watching their grandchildren play around their arthritic old feet. They're still young at heart, driving them around in superminis labelled 'the Grancan'. Or they're taking them skiing, swimming or camping, when they're not taking time off work for a holiday spent trekking in the Himalayas. And there's the 75 year old I know whose idea of fun is free-fall parachuting in the Cook Islands....

Here's an extract from Joy, a 10 year old writing about her grandparents. She includes a snippet about her greatgrandparent, still actively entertaining Joy's grandparents.

"Sometimes for a treat we go round for tea and Pops goes to pick up a Chinese for us all. Nana always spoils us and gives us sweets. I like walking the dog with Pops; if we go to the beach and it's warm enough he lets me paddle in the sea. My great-nana is 93, but she's still very independent and still makes marmalade. She makes lunch for Nana and Pops every Friday."

Grandparents – even greatgrandparents – are much fitter, healthier and younger in heart today. The child who wrote: "Grandmothers wear glasses and funny underwear. They can take their teeth and gums out." had an unusual experience of grandparents. Today, grandchildren usually arrive long before infirmity does.

"I like going fishing and swimming with my Grandad. My

sister was fishing with me and my Grandad. She caught three fish." *Danielle, age 10*

When do Grandchildren Arrive?

There's no ideal age to be a grandparent – for any age it's a wonderful joy. Nearly a quarter of our grandparents had their first grandchild *before* they were 50, clearly fit and active. Most of the grandparents in our survey had their first grandchild when they were in their fifties – indeed national surveys show that half of today's grandparents are in their fifties or younger. But although better health makes for better grandparenting, youthfulness may not, for various reasons. Some of our grandparents made thoughtful comments on this question of age and grandparenthood. One or two of them explained why being a young grandparent isn't always an advantage, illustrated by the following comment:

> "I'm so busy with my own work and other activities that I can't play the part I want to play with my grandchild. I feel I'm missing out on something very precious."

If you're young enough to enjoy your grandchildren, you may also be young enough to be working, and perhaps contributing to your local community too. Today, there are so many more opportunities for women to work than there used to be.

There is a different situation that's quite the reverse of the one just described, yet has the same effect of preventing grandparents today from fully enjoying their grandchildren. That is the tendency for young women to delay having children until they are, by previous standards, older mothers. So one grandmother, who had her first grandchild in her seventies, wrote:

> "So many women today are having babies in their late thirties or early forties that some grandmothers are in their sixties

and seventies, which makes it much harder physically to look after small children, however much they want to."

That comment was echoed by a grandfather, whose four grandchildren had arrived when he was in his sixties. He wrote:

"Certainly we wouldn't have wanted ours at any later age. The sheer physical exuberance of toddlers and infants is quite a challenge, even in your sixties."

And yet another thought. Today, many more young people live and work at a distance, or even abroad, and so some grandparents won't be able to see their grandchildren as much as they might like for reasons of distance. Even if you're young at heart and fit and have the time, there may still be other obstacles to be overcome.

These are three examples of some of the changes in society that may prevent some grandparents from enjoying their grandchildren as much as they might have hoped. So while it's probably right to assume that grandparents today are usually well enough to be able to enjoy their grandchildren more than in previous generations, our changing society may raise difficulties for them.

So, to summarise:

- Grandparents are no longer problems, they're assets.

- Today, grandparenthood doesn't mean collapsing into old age.

- You'll probably be fit enough to play an active part in your grandchild's life.

- If circumstances prevent this, consider your priorities:
  - If you're working, could you alter your work pattern?
  - If you're not working but still active, could you lose some responsibilities?

- We may be able to choose when we want to be parents: we certainly can't choose when we want to be grandparents. But we have to bear in mind that what we had always expected and hoped to do for the new arrival might well be limited by our circumstances when the grandchild arrives.

CHAPTER 3

Appreciating Grandparents

"Everybody should try to have a grandparent, especially if they don't have television, because they are the only grown-ups who like to spend time with us."

Busier Parents

The changed relationship between women and employment, mentioned in the last chapter, has altered the pattern of family life. In many families with young children today, both parents work. Who looks after the young children; who spends time with them?

The first thought is often "What about my Mum – could she help?" But not only are grandparents younger and fitter, they too may be working or living at a distance. Yet many grandparents today do indeed provide some or much of the childcare support that enables the parents to work. This is another way in which today's grandparents differ from yesterday's, when most mothers stayed at home and cared for their children themselves. It's a situation that can be delicate to deal with, and it's discussed in Chapter 7.

In real life, surveys show that most grandparents see their children at least once a week; contact is much more frequent than is usually imagined. Sometimes, of course, family circumstances lead to an even closer link. But for most grandchildren, the link with their grandparents is reinforced by regular visits. If regular visits aren't possible, what then?

Technology Support

Not only are grandparents probably busier than formerly, their families are far more widely scattered: children move away from their parents; some move overseas. How can grandparents with families like these fit their distant grandchildren into their busy daily lives? Do these active, working grandparents manage to see much of their grandchildren? Or do they see them on holidays only? Where grandchildren are scattered, and far away, letters, phone calls, e-mails, all enable grandparents and the most distant grandchildren to keep in close and immediate touch.

It's easy to forget how technology-minded our grandchildren are. They grow up in a world where modern technology is taken for granted. I can recall the trepidation with which my parents approached the arrival of a telephone in the house. Making calls was something reserved for parents. Later, after they had mastered the beast, I had to be taught how to answer the phone, and later how to dial. Today, phoning is taken for granted in the great majority of homes: the telephone is almost a toy, which children play with.

"No Emily, do put the phone down; it's not something to chew."

Today, dial-up phones are old technology to our grandchildren. Our grandchildren live in a world where communication, by text, by voice, by picture, even, is being done through mobile phones. Computers, which we struggled to come to terms with, are everyday tools to the young, not only sources of information for school projects. They are ways for grandson to send Grandad shots of the fish he caught, or for granddaughter to send Gran a picture of her new party dress. We'd better learn to keep up.

Of course, we're trying hard. Over half of us in our sixties and seventies own a mobile phone. And the 'silver surfers' are busy on their keyboards, trying hard to negotiate the internet. But owning modern technology is not the same as using it. We need to be helped. And who will help us? Our grandchildren, of course.

"Just go into the *edit* menu Grandma and click on *select all.*"

"Thank you, Emily: how would I manage without you?"

But communication with grandchildren isn't always simple and enjoyable. According to the Family Policy Study Centre, the growing divorce rate means that soon over a quarter of school children will have to cope with divorce in the family. What does this mean for grandparenting? What kind of roles do grandparents and step-grandparents play in these changed situations? And what about adoptive grandparents? For many families, grandparenting can involve intricate relationships, communication can become complicated and we touch on some of these issues in Chapter 17.

Grandparents are Important

In my boyhood, I had had 14 uncles and aunts in my family. Four had died, either in childhood or in the Great War, four had moved away, but six uncles and aunts lived within a couple of miles of my house, in easy walking distance. Help when a new child arrived was always at hand, if the mother wanted it.

Today's families are not only more scattered; they are smaller and busier. Uncles and aunts aren't usually as available to help as they once were. Grandparents, on the other hand, are fitter, live longer, are more active, and are younger in outlook. So they are more important players in the family set-up than they used to be, often helping to provide the childcare that keeps the economy of family and nation afloat. Even if they're distant from their grandchildren, they're still significant characters in the grandchildren's lives, offering stability when times are turbulent.

Is our growing role appreciated? Attitudes to grandparents and grandparenting are certainly changing in line with the changing times.

In the USA they have an official 'Grandparents' Day'. It's the first Sunday after Labor Day, a day selected in 1978 by President Jimmy Carter. And grandparents are really celebrated in style, with National Grandparents of the year being elected across the States. Yes, grandparents are BIG NEWS there. And in Italy, as I write, a bill giving the Italians a grandparents' day is in its final stages. The Italian Grandparents' Day will be on October 2nd, which whether by accident or design, happens to be the Catholic feast day of Guardian Angels. What a nice touch. We're Guardian Angels.

In this country, we've begun to follow a more practical approach to appreciating the new grandparents. Sixty percent of childcare provision is said to be provided by grandparents, and economists have tried to work out the value of this unpaid childcare. It's a huge sum – over four billion pounds per annum – and there have been moves to find ways of acknowledging this through payments. Pressure groups, demanding rights for grandparents over delicate matters of access to grandchildren have sprung up. No longer are grandparents seen as threats to the happy family; our roles have changed. Our significance to modern family life is being acknowledged as never before, and in the chapters that follow, grandparents themselves outline some of the traditional pleasures that grandparenting still offers, and some of the skills needed to avoid the pitfalls of the new role.

So, to summarise:

- Reaching grandparenthood is no longer a sign of approaching decrepitude: you've acquired a new, important status. Get ready for it.

- Your children are probably going to need you again.

- Be prepared for a request to help a busy family.

- Don't underestimate little children's facility for communicating with new technology.

- So unless you're an expert, take a course to improve your skills with computers, mobile phones and any other new technology.

CHAPTER 4

Great News

Anxious father rings the hospital: "You must help: my wife's just gone into labour."

Nurse: "Calm down. Is this her first child?"

Anxious father: "No, it's her husband."

Grandchild Arrives

Of course they're anxious, and so are you, even though you've been there before. Now, like them, you're waiting for the really big moment, the moment when the baby arrives. You've been running to the phone every day for weeks – just in case it's *the* phone call. At last it comes...

"It's a boy – or girl, X kilos." Yes, it might just be in metric measurements, so be prepared. These days hospitals record weights in kilos, which is the first reminder that you're from an older generation, when these things were done differently, and babies were measured in the old weights. But most hospitals will also have translated the kilos into pounds and ounces, so the new parents can tell you the weight in familiar terms.

"How's mother?" you ask immediately. And once you've been reassured, you may well want to rush over to see the new arrival at once, for this is *the* time when grandparents, especially grandmothers, are needed more than at any other occasion.

Be careful: if the mother is your own daughter, you're pretty sure she will want to see you as soon as possible, both at the hospital and to help in the home. But not always; some new mothers just want to enjoy their baby, and don't want to be mothered them-selves. Relationships can change in different ways when grand-children are born. And if the mother is your daughter-in-law, be even more sensitive. You may have to learn to play second fiddle at this moment: but handle it tactfully now and your rewards will come later. It might be much better to ask how soon could you see the baby.

What to Give

You want to mark the occasion of course. It's a real event in the family, in *your* family. You'll probably think of giving something for the parents and, more importantly, something for the baby. What should you give?

Gifts are very personal matters, and the comments that follow may be quite different from your own views.

For the parents it's usually not too difficult. Most mothers would love a huge bunch of flowers. There'll probably be other flowers from other family members, but that doesn't matter. The box of cigars for Dad has long disappeared, but he ought to have some-thing, even if it's just a bottle of his favourite tipple. Get him involved from the start.

But you may want to give something more substantial for the new family. If so, ask the parents what they want to start things off, if only to avoid duplicating gifts; a baby buggy perhaps, or a cot. Something that can be used again for any later children is always a good idea.

Something for Grandchild

But what about the baby? You may want to rush out and settle money on the baby now, something that might help towards their later education, or for helping towards a deposit, when they might eventually think of buying a house. But be careful. That's an understandably generous reaction, but pause; what you do for one, you'll want to do for all. Remember what was said earlier: you can control the number of your children, but not of your grandchildren, so best hold that decision for a while. (We discuss money matters in Chapter 8.)

What you can do is give something personal to the baby. Grandfathers may think of pewter drinking tankards for the baby to use later. Not really such a good idea now: later perhaps. But a small apostle spoon, a silver cup, something personal, preferably with the child's name on it – this is the kind of keep-sake that often gives pleasure to parents now and the child later.

Many grandmothers used to knit a baby garment, and – if you have the time and inclination – that's nearly always very accept-able, not least because it's something that was made by your own hand, always a sign of particular love and care. Grandfathers can do something similar – a personalised piece of child's furniture – perhaps a chair or a stool, for example. But if you're not into crafts, there are many other possibilities; the list is endless, and the choice is yours. How about laying down some wine, to be enjoyed when both baby and gift have matured: a bottle of port – or even a case? Or a framed family tree, designed by an artist? Or a cuddly toy – anything from a simple bunny rabbit to a Steiff teddy bear?

How about a golden sovereign, dated the year of birth? Or a pre-mium bond or two – who knows, it might be a very profitable gift indeed? Or might the baby might become a collector later? If so a few collectables to start him or her off would be interesting. If it's a girl, some grandparents like to give a small piece of jewellery, perhaps a bangle.

We gave framed samplers with the baby's name, date of birth, and various designs to each of our grandchildren, apart from two, where mother wanted samplers made from a relative on her own side of the family. Fortunately we'd checked beforehand and so we gave something else.

This draws attention to another point: do check with the parents first before deciding. Other family members may have the same idea, and no child will want half-a-dozen stools, even if they're different designs.

And you may want to mark the occasion for yourself, perhaps by planting a tree in the garden, something to bring pleasant associations over the years. But remember, you may end up with a small forest.

Personalised gifts raise the question of the new arrival's name. Perhaps the parents are still thinking about a name, and you'd like to know in order to have it engraved on your piece of presentation glass or whatever.

Don't try to hurry them over the name; they'll decide in their own time. And whatever you do, don't try to persuade them that it would be nice to have Grandad's family name perpetuated, or Uncle Archibald Eustace commemorated. Uncle Archibald Eustace may be a millionaire bachelor with no other relatives in sight. But no child is going to enjoy confessing to monikers like that all his life, especially when, after a family tiff, Archibald Eustace finally leaves his millions to the local dogs' home. The parents must choose the names themselves, and you must applaud the choice, no matter how revolting or impossible you think they are. After all, it can't be worse than the parents who called their twins Kate and Duplicate.

Why give anything personal right now? Some grandparents feel the buggy, or some other useful gift, is the most appropriate thought now, and think of the christening, or naming ceremony, as the event they'd like to mark with a personal gift that the baby will cherish in years to come. After all, they must have a name by a naming ceremony... The choice – birth, or christening, or both – is yours.

But these days you can't assume that there will have to be a christening or naming ceremony; the parents may not want either. In that event, have a quiet word with the parents about your wish to commemorate the new arrival.

What Name for Yourself?

Children generally call people by the name they've heard others use. So if you're willing for your grandchildren to call you by your first name, that's fine. Indeed there seems to be a growing trend for children to do just that and for grandparents to be happy with it.

If you prefer to be called by a different name, one that shows your relationship more clearly, do let your family know in good time the name you'd like to have used. So choose your new identity, and remember that consistency is helpful for little ones.

If two sets of grandparents like the same name, they can easily be differentiated by place: Nana London and Nana Bristol, for example. Or grandchildren may coin their own terms, usually honestly accurate: Big Pop and Little Pop, for example. Unless it really distresses you (Podgy, perhaps?), grin and bear it.

When the grandchildren first try to get their tongues round your chosen name, all sorts of variants can appear, and if you reinforce their efforts with an amused smile, the variants are liable to stick. Here are some of the many different names that we've heard being used.

Grandfathers	**Grandmothers**
Granddad	Grandma
Grandpapa	Grandmama
Grandpa	Gran
Granpop	Granny
Grandy	Lala
Pop	Mamgu (South Wales)
Pop-pop	Nan
Grumps	Nana
Papa	Nanny
Poppa	Nain (North Wales)
Popsy	Tante
Taid (North Wales)	
Tadcu (South Wales)	

If you're interested in a wider selection, there are sites on the internet (e.g. thenewparentsguide.com) that offer longer lists, including names used in other countries.

So, to summarise:

● Don't rush to see the baby until you've found out when it's convenient.

● Choose an appropriate gift.

● Don't even drop the slightest hint about names.

● Take or send something for mother.

● And something for father.

● And consider marking such an important milestone with a gift to yourself.

● Let the family know what you'd like to be called.

CHAPTER 5

Changing Relationships

"...how wonderful to see my own daughter change into becoming a good mother: fantastic!"

Relationships with the Grandchild

Children change when your grandchildren are born, and so do you. The change begins when you hold your grandchild for the first time. For those grandmothers who answered our questionnaire, holding the first grandchild was the most pleasurable experience of all. Grandfathers enjoyed it too, but were more pleased with later experiences, like playing with the grandchildren and having them to stay. But whether you're a grandmother or grandfather, be prepared for that rush of feeling when you cradle that warm little bundle of babyhood in your arms for the first time. It brings back so many emotions from your days of being a parent of young children, and new feelings too.

"Don't drop it, Grandad," someone's sure to say; as if you would.

Of course, human beings vary; not all of us cherish the same experiences. For one New Zealand grandmother, the moment that beat even holding her first grandchild came a couple of years later, when she took that first grandchild to see his newly arrived brother. The look of pure wonder on his face was something she could never forget.

This new life, your new grandchild, is the person with whom you form the most important new relationship. Holding the child for the first time starts the bonding process. You hold the child, feel the wriggles, smell the baby smell, hear the crying, encounter the tenderness towards such a helpless bundle and you begin to realise you've suddenly crossed a frontier. You've entered new territory, the land of grandparenthood, and you're making a new relationship. You've heard so much about it from friends and relatives, and now you're going to experience it for yourself. It's going to affect you in different ways.

It's not the same relationship as that you made with your own children when they were young. You'll rightly look forward to being able to savour again some of those experiences you enjoyed then – playing with the children, reading to them, teasing them – in short, reliving some of your earlier years. Yet, as one grandmother wrote, relationships with grandchildren are really quite different; more relaxed, more fun, less responsibility.

Relationships within the Family

But the new arrival affects other relationships too, sometimes immediately obviously, but sometimes in quite subtle ways. Part of the pleasure you get from the new family structure comes from the changed relationship with your own son or daughter. One grandfather wrote how much he enjoyed seeing the pleasure his own children had from being parents, and thriving on parenthood.

Another grandfather wrote in the same vein:

> "There has been on my part a great appreciation of my changed relationship with the new parental generation in my family – all six of them!"

This includes the changed relationship with your in-laws, too, something that several grandmothers mentioned. One grandfather wrote:

> "It's a shock realising that one's own son-in-law is now a permanent fixture – I mean for ever. By some curious process of

osmosis he and I have become related and now share something for ever. Not that I have a problem with that, but nobody prepared me for it."

This new relationship works both ways. Your children are now living the experiences you experienced, perhaps 30 or so years ago, and this often gives them a proper insight into all you did for them, all those years ago. Unexpected emotions like appreciation and even gratitude begin to flow. Enjoy them – it's nice to be appreciated. But don't wallow in them; remember that swollen heads burst haloes.

Yet there are always shadows for some. One grandmother had a different reaction from most. She wrote:

"Seeing the way your daughter or son is bringing up their child will probably question your own child-rearing methods. Guilt may occur."

This was one of the very few mentions of guilt from any grandparent, but it's worth being aware of it. Others may have thought it, but not been willing to confess to it, of course.

The more frequent comment on modern child-rearing was surprise, probably mixed with some shock and horror. Your children are now, as was said earlier, becoming experts on child-rearing. They may still turn to you, but there's a subtle change: your view is now more an opinion to be considered, rather than a rule to be followed.

Best accept that there are differences between then and now. Times are different, children are brought up in a different era now, and while many child-rearing skills are timeless, they may have to be adapted to changing circumstances. To take an example, your own rules about bedtimes may well be quite different from those your children might want for the grandchildren. Relax! You did well with your own children and be sure that your children will do well with theirs. Even if you're horrified at the regime they've adopted, and the three year old is running around the lounge creating mayhem at 10 at night, say nothing: don't even raise an eyebrow.

Relationships with the Other Grandparents

So far we've talked about your new grandchild as if you are the only grandparents, and have sole grandparenting rights. Not so. There is usually at least one other couple of grandparents who bear the same relationship to the new arrival as you do and, these days, perhaps several more. Some of our grandparents said that this relationship required skill to handle, and a few said that it gave pleasure. So it's a relationship that needs some care. There's potential for rivalry here, and that's to be avoided.

"Try not to compete with the other grandparents," one grandfather wrote. "You are what you are."

Much may depend on accessibility of course. If you happen to be living 10 minutes away and the other set of grandparents are at the other end of the country, or even abroad, you're bound to see much more of the grandchild than they do. Which means that when they do come to visit, you hang back: let them have their turn – you've been having yours all year.

For most – though not all – new mothers, the most important figures in the older generation are her own mother and father. Sometimes relationships with mother and father are not good, and so sometimes circumstances mean that there are others, perhaps a favourite aunt and uncle, to whom the new mother turns. Rarely is it the parents-in-law. Most new parents want to involve both sets of grandparents in the new arrival's life, but do be just a little careful if you're the mother's in-laws. Mother-in-law jokes are not so prevalent without good reason.

One or two grandparents may feel that their daughter-in-law is denying them the access to the grandchild that they feel they deserve and need. Perhaps you feel that the other grandparents are being favoured at your expense.

Don't ignore the problem. Be nice to your daughter-in-law: a little present perhaps, or an invitation out? Relationships have to be worked on. And when the moment is ripe, talk with her about your feelings.

There are many positives to be gained from the relationship with the other grandparents. They're probably from the same generation as you, have had similar life experiences, may enjoy the same hobbies and pastimes. So you have a lot in common – not least a new grandchild. But get to know them for themselves, not only as fellow-grandparents.

My own mother and mother-in-law were very wary of each other at first. Once our first child – their grandchild – was born, they started to see much more of each other, and a few years later were going on bridge cruises together. When that first child in turn became a parent, he and his wife insisted that both sets of grandparents joined the new family for holidays, and later, we and the other grandparents were staying at each other's houses for beach and bowls holidays.

Getting to know the other grandparents is an opportunity to make new friends. Let the friendship develop at its own rate and in its own way, but be determined that this new relationship, like the others, shall be positive, a relationship of friendship, not rivalry.

So, to summarise:

- Holding your new grandchild is a wonderfully emotional experience.

- Recognise that having a grandchild is not like having a child; it's more relaxing, less stressful, and with fewer responsibilities.

- Seeing your own children as parents is a fascinating education.

- Be prepared to work hard on the relationship with your daughter-in-law or son-in-law.

- And also with any other grandparents.

- Share what you have in common with the other grandparents, as well as sharing the grandchildren.

CHAPTER 6

Poor Advice and Wise Counsel

"Advice? Never give it!" (comment from a grandfather)

The Family Sage

Once you're a grandparent you begin to realise that you're the possessor of skills and knowledge that could well be in demand. Your children, now parents themselves, begin to see the world in terms of the continuity of the generations. They begin to ask questions about earlier days that only you can answer.

"Dad, didn't you once say something about an uncle who had red hair like little Oliver?"

And so you have the opportunity to reveal long obscured details of family history to pass on to your children, who've now developed an interest in matters that previously hadn't excited them. You're the possessor of the family archives, the keeper of its oral history. Enjoy the new dignity that your role of grandparent has conferred on you, and pass the information on.

"Oh yes: that was my uncle Ben. Made a fortune, went to gaol for embezzlement, and ended up driving a milk float part time for one of the dairy chains. That was when he wasn't on social security. Looked just like Oliver."

"Oh."

Idea Store Bow

1 Gladstone Place, Roman Road, London E3 5ES

020-7364-4332   www.ideastore.co.uk

ITEMS ISSUED/RENEWED

FOR Mrs Lola Ogunsola

ON 09/07/11 16:03:29

AT Idea Store Bow (TH)

Insider's guide to being a brilliant 8/W

C001532607   DUE 30/07/11

1 item(s) issued

The Child-rearing Expert

Another aspect of your new status is your experience of child-rearing. You've been there, done it, encountered and overcome all the big and little worries about raising children, so you may find your experience in some demand. The chance to help a new parent who's in the middle of a huge, life-changing experience is one of the pleasures of being a grandparent. It helps to create a special bond. To new parents, little worries can easily become large ones.

"Mum, little Oliver won't eat his greens. How did you get me to eat cabbage?"

"I didn't, dear. I tried very hard, but you wouldn't touch it. In fact you lived on Kit-Kats for over a year, and it hasn't damaged you, has it?" (Or, more seriously, try mixing the greens with something else; or give fruit instead, it's a healthy alternative. You might even give your son or daughter a copy of White Ladder Press's book **The Art of Hiding Vegetables** *Sneaky ways to feed your children healthy food* £7.99.)

A request for your help is one thing: unsolicited advice is quite another. In the opinions of the grandparents we consulted, giving advice to the parents on child-rearing was far and away the situation that most grandmothers and grandfathers thought required skill. It was the one situation that evoked more comments than any other. It clearly touched a sensitive spot. The comments ranged from:

"It's not skill that's needed in giving advice, but diplomacy."

Through: "I think it's very important not to interfere when the parents are doing something that you feel is not the right way to handle a situation. By all means help, but be careful not to *tell* them what to do."

To short and sweet: "Just don't."

Of course there may well be emergencies when you feel you have to interfere for the sake of the child. There's Oliver, aged two, who's suddenly found that lovely shiny kitchen knife, and doesn't want to hand it over. The more Mum tries to take it from him, the more firmly he clutches it to him, becoming perilously close to severing an artery. You jump in at once, offering him a sweet, a toy, anything else that might entice him to drop the knife in exchange. There are so many of the little tricks of managing children that you've learnt over the years, but which your children have yet to learn.

But in non-emergencies – and that means nearly all situations – grandparents all warned against giving unsolicited advice, or at the very least, being very, very diplomatic over how you offer it. As one grandmother wrote:

> "Knowing when to give advice, when to care without undermining the parents – that needs a lot of skill on the grandparents' part."

That point about undermining the parents is particularly one to watch if the parents themselves hold different views about aspects of child-rearing. After all, the parents have been brought up in different families, so it would be surprising if they held identical views – about discipline for example. Perhaps they turn to Gran or Grandad for an opinion about who's right.

"I don't think Dad ought to smack little Oliver when he won't finish his food. What do you think Grandad?"

Watch it! If you please one parent, you'll probably antagonise the other. The parents have to work out a common approach themselves, and if they differ, they must try to compromise. If you're asked to be a referee, remember that referees are neutral, forget your own thoughts and encourage them to agree for the sake of little Oliver. A united approach in the family on key matters like discipline and boundaries is very important for children. Usually two parents agreeing, even over what you feel strongly is the wrong approach, is better for the child than one parent holding the right approach and the other disagreeing. There's no harm in gently reminding them of that.

Changes in Child-rearing

We grandparents have to bear in mind that patterns and systems of child-rearing change. For example, who today recalls the Plunkett system, a rigid feeding schedule for infants, imported from New Zealand and very popular from the 1920s to the 1950s. Bottles were allowed only at strict four hour intervals, and babies had to wait until the clock struck the hour. In between, no feeding was allowed, no matter how much the infant cried. Attitudes changed afterwards and a more tolerant, laissez-faire approach followed: new generations introduce new ideas.

Twenty-first century views on bringing up children will differ again in various ways from those you followed in raising your children. Dr. Spock is being superseded, and a regular regime is becoming popular again with many parents. Your children may seem to you to be slaves of strange fads and practices: it may be hard to bite your tongue and avoid commenting, but better a sore tongue than a resentful or angry parent. Don't try to put the clock back: times are different now, even though they may not be better. After all, if there was one best way to bring up children, those myriad parents who have brought up children across the years would surely have found it by now.

Take another example: grandfathers love helping their grandchildren to read. You may shake your head at the way young Oliver, now six, struggles over the words in his reading book. Don't try to teach him the way you learnt to read. You *think* it's the way you learnt, but it may not be – grandparents' memories are notoriously patchy. And even if it is the way you learnt, why try to impose it on Oliver? The last thing to do is to confuse him; just let him struggle on with working out the names of the letters, or whatever heresy he seems to you to be following. It's what teacher says, and teacher, to Oliver, is right. He'll get there in the end, even if his route seems strange and tortuous to you.

Your role is not that of teacher or parent; you're the grandparent. It's a different role, and one to make the most of and to enjoy.

So, to summarise:

- The birth of a grandchild often sparks off an interest in your knowledge of family history, so brush it up. Perhaps prepare a family tree, or record your own childhood memories.

- It also sparks an interest in your experience of child-rearing. If you're asked for advice, remember that 'giving advice' to the new parents is a highly charged issue, so be diplomatic.

- Remember that different generations march to different tunes. Always think of Harry Truman, who said "I have found that the best way to give advice to your children is to find out what they want to do, then tell them to do it."

- If the parents differ over child-rearing, don't take sides, even if you're sure one is right and the other wrong.

- Children are taught differently from when you were in school. So don't interfere with the school's teaching methods. Help in harmony with the school.

CHAPTER 7

To Care or Not to Care

"I'm glad you've come, Gran." (Gran was Joshua's Mum's mother.)

Why, Joshua?"

"I want to see Daddy do his trick."

"What's that, Joshua?"

"I heard him promise Mummy that next time you came he'd climb up the wall."

Respite Care

While grandparenthood brings pleasure, it also brings responsibilities. Apart from the question of a regular commitment to helping the parents with the grandchildren, there will be times when you feel that you want to offer to have the children for a little while. Willingness to offer a little 'respite care', to enable tired parents to recharge the batteries, is something that parents greatly appreciate.

And of course there are times when even the best of marriages goes through a stressful period. That's another time when grandparents can offer a brief space, taking temporary charge of the grandchildren while the parents put their relationship back on an even keel.

Being able to offer occasional help at difficult times is one of the joys of grandparenthood. Yes, it may mean altering your routine, perhaps giving up that regular Tuesday lunch or that bridge evening, but do so; it's a duty that brings many rewards.

Some grandparents loved it: the chance of reliving their own days of looking after children, of using their own skills of child-rearing again – for them this was a wonderful opportunity. One grandmother wrote:

> "I particularly enjoy being able to help at vital moments, e.g. when the child's mother is very tired, or when the parents simply need a change of scene."

Others were much less happy about it. A grandmother said:

> "It's hard to refuse requests to look after my young grandchildren when the parents need help. But I brought up my own three children as a single mother, and now when I've retired from work and at last I'm looking forward to some years without responsibilities, the grandchildren have come along. I love the grandchildren, and I never refuse requests for help. Yet I can't help feeling it's a bit of an imposition; and then I feel guilty for thinking that."

And there was the grandmother who felt that the best part of helping with her grandchild was the knowledge that she could give the child back afterwards, and her responsibilities would end.

Another grandmother touched on a different kind of emotional issue; your place in the grandchild's affections.

> "After caring for your grandchild all day, accept that they will ignore you and turn to the parents the moment they arrive home."

Other grandparents have found that occasional requests for help with the grandchildren can grow until they approach a regular commitment, and even become unbearable. One grandparent couple actually moved house to the other end of the country in order to avoid the frequent calls for help from the parents.

That's an extreme example, of course, but it does drive the point home.

Being asked to help in little ways, like meeting your grandchild after school, or when an unexpected need arises – perhaps when a grandchild of school age is ill and can't be left alone, or when a caring arrangement breaks down temporarily – is quite different from a more permanent arrangement.

Offering regular and consistent help with childcare for your new grandchild is definitely something else, something to be considered very carefully.

A Commitment to Care

In the UK we have one of the highest percentages of female workers in Europe. Many of these women are mothers, often with young children. The days when married women rarely held jobs or, if they did, waited to return to work until their children were old enough to manage on their own in the day, have long since gone. Today, most mothers, like fathers, expect and want to be able to work, including mothers of young children. Of course there's legislation requiring employers to provide leave for new parents, both mothers and fathers, so that in the immediate aftermath of little Tamsin's arrival, the demands of work don't interfere with those of parenthood. But when the period of leave ends: what then? Some arrangement has to be made for little Tamsin to be looked after while the parents are at work.

Where one of the parents earns a good income, couples may want to arrange matters so that the other partner gives up the job to become for the time being a full time housewife or househusband. Or the parents may be able to arrange for both to work part time.

Yet many couples prefer to keep both jobs, perhaps because the income is important for them or perhaps because both enjoy their work. Between them, the parents may earn enough to pay for childcare in the day; some may even be able to afford a nanny. In those circumstances, the problems of childcare are greatly reduced. But not everyone can afford that Rolls-Royce level of care. So in most situations some arrangement has to be made, and a carer has to be found. Grandparents!

Grandparents can be trusted, they know the child, and they may not be living too far away: in a national survey 60% of grandparents saw one of their grandchildren at least once a week. Not all grandchildren are as close as Sian, aged 10, who wrote:

> "I live very close to both grandparents. One Nana and Grandad live next door, and the others are across the road from the school."

Even if grandparents live far away, they can be asked to come and stay. "Why even think of paying for professional childcare from someone who's a stranger, while Gran and Grandad are available?" the parents ask. And if you're pensioners, who've retired from work, you'll have lots of spare time, they think. Why, you actually need an interest to fill your empty days, they imagine. Dream on, you murmur, thinking rapidly of your bridge club, the whist drives, the over fifties club, U3A, the gardening association, the bowls club, that driving you do for the elderly, the badminton morning, the NSPCC committee, the ...*stop*! So you're asked to help with looking after little Tamsin. Should you say 'yes'?

This question of being a regular carer for working parents was one of the more prominent concerns of the grandparents in our survey. Some of the issues they mentioned are highlighted below.

First, be prepared in case you're asked to help. Even before little Tamsin arrives, it's as well to think how much help you're wanting, and will be able, to give. And if you're unsure how much you're able to help, perhaps it's better to think smaller rather than larger at first. When you're used to your new responsibilities you'll be able to decide whether you can offer more; and an increased offer of help is always much more acceptable than a forced reduction, however reluctantly made.

Then think carefully about the commitment. What of your activities might you have to give up? What difference would it make to your social life and to your friendships? And think about the responsibility. Little children can be a responsibility, as you well know.

> "I remember being naughty and running out of my Gran's house into the road, wearing only nappies, and Gran was cross." *Sophie, aged 10*

> "I used to smash glasses in posh restaurants. I used to do a poo when my Gran changed my nappy." *Tom, aged 10*

Consider these three questions carefully.

1 Are you going to be happy with little Tamsin arriving as mother shoots off to work each morning, and then looking after your grandchild until father arrives for the evening pick up?

2 Are you going to feel resentful at the thought that you are doing this to enable two incomes to pour into your children's household, while you manage on what may well be a mean little pension?

3 Are you going to be hurt when, after caring all day for your grandchild, the moment Mum and Dad come home, little Tamsin ignores you and turns to the parents?

If you can put your hand on your heart and say a firm 'yes' to the first question, and an equally firm 'no' to the second and third, then congratulations. You're tailor-made for the role of carer.

Trying it Out

If you have doubts, if you feel uneasy about taking on the responsibilities of looking after a young child again, or if you feel, like one of the grandparents above, that you want this time of your life to be your time, to do what you've never been able to do before, then don't say 'yes', even though you feel you ought to. Perhaps offer a trial period before deciding. Then if you find it's too much, give the parents enough time to work out alternative arrangements before you back out.

One of the snags of a trial period is the difficulty of backing out, even though you've made your intentions clear from the start. So instead of offering a full time trial, you could always offer a part time trial, say a half-day or a full day once a week. You may find that a good way of starting off. Or you might enjoy offering to try a specific role, like the grandfather who wrote:

> "One of my greatest pleasures is meeting my small grandson from school every day. We really get to know each other."

Saying no to being a regular, committed carer, either full time or part time, doesn't rule out helping occasionally, when the situation demands. One willing grandmother added her own conditions:

> "I'll always help if you're stuck, dear, but not on Thursdays unless there's a real emergency. It's the golf day, and I'll have arrangements to cancel."

The Residential Granny-nanny

There is another side to this question of caring. Some grandparents, particularly grandmothers, really feel very strongly that if the parents are both determined to work they, the grandparents, have a duty to look after their grandchild. Better to look after little Tamsin themselves, rather than let the parents use the services of strangers running a creche, they think. So they offer to come and live with the parents, and be an unpaid residential nanny.

It's an offer the parents may find hard to refuse; it solves all their problems of child care at a stroke. But if you feel like making such a generous offer, do think about your motives. Are you doing this for little Tamsin and the parents, or for yourself? And who will be running the household? What effect will this situation have on your relationship with mother? You may well feel that having a full time 'nanny' at home –yourself – looking after little Tamsin during the day, is a much more attractive arrangement than placing her in a creche or nursery school. But you're not a nanny – you're the grandmother, and that's very different.

So in short, carefully think through this issue of helping with care. There are good reasons why experienced grandmothers felt this situation needed real skill to handle. And it's worth emphasising again that it's much easier to increase your caring commitment, rather than cut it down, when there may be possible recriminations as the parents' expectations are reduced.

So, to summarise:

- This was a contentious question.

- When both parents work, grandparents are often an obvious source of child-care.

- Be prepared: think carefully beforehand about what help you can offer.

- In particular, remember that despite the great rewards in the relationship you build with your grandchild:
  - little children are responsibilities;
  - the amount of childcare you offer may affect your income and your social life;
  - you can never replace the parents in the child's eyes.

● Most grandparents enjoyed helping over occasional emergencies.

● It's easier to increase help than to cut back, so consider a part time trial of a regular commitment, or offering an easy regular task at first.

● Think very hard before living with your children as a full time nanny.

CHAPTER 8

Money and All That

"I am very fond of the diamond watch that my grandmother sold me on her deathbed."

That's a Woody Allen line that does raise the question of how best to help the grandchildren.

"What's the best way of making financial arrangements for my grandchildren's future?" That's a question we thought would concern many of our grandparents. While some of our group felt that it was an important issue, they were fewer than expected. In discussion, the main reason for this emerged: many grandparents felt that they'd leave the grandchildren 'something in the will'. That would take care of the matter.

> "Why commit some money now, when no one knows how much I may need for my own old age? The cost of nursing homes is so high that I feel I have to make sure I'm as well protected as possible."

That was a fairly popular view. Yet there were a few grandparents who felt they actually enjoyed making arrangements for the grandchildren's future. It gave them a feeling of pleasure that they had helped the youngest members of the family to a good start in life.

Why Help?

Why set money aside at all? Why not just leave it in the will? Well, hopefully your will won't be read until your grandchildren are mature adults, and many grandparents feel that it's most important for young people to get a helping hand as early in life as possible. Who better to help to a good start than your own grandchildren? Forget your worries about the profligate young spending your money on raves on the beach in Cancun, or subsidising a hippy commune in the South Seas, or buying Ferraris. Let's assume they're too wise for that – they're not the grandchildren of spendthrift George IVth, who spent £24,000 on just one of the robes for his coronation. They're yours, so they're bound to be sensible, thoughtful, shrewd, generous, etc etc, just like you. What might they use a nest egg for? Here are a few examples.

- Starting a business.

- Gaining a higher education qualification without the worries of a large loan to repay.

- Putting a deposit on a house.

- Or you may belong to a family that believes in independent schools, and the parents can't quite afford the fees.

There are endless ways in which a small amount of capital can help your grandchildren do something that otherwise would be denied them.

Financial experts love threatening us with estimates of the costs young people may have to face. Here are some of them:

- University education – say £7,000 per annum for at least three years.

- First home – say £120,000.

- Wedding – say £14,000.

- And if the parents want a fee paying education, the estimate for that is somewhere between £90,000 and £190,000.

Of course these are all crude sums, ballpark figures that rise every year, and individual costs will vary tremendously. Forget the details. The important point is that little Thomas and his brothers and sisters will appreciate any help you can provide in order for them to get a good start in life. Let's assume you'd like to help.

How to Help

How best to do this? Those who had done so, had used a small fraction only of the various ways of helping grandchildren during the grandparents' lifetime.

Give a Lump Sum Now

Perhaps the simplest way is to invest a sum of money in the grandchild's name. This is a clear cut arrangement, and of course it's financially advantageous in that, provided the grandchild's total income falls below the taxable minimum, no tax is payable. Some grandparents do just this.

What a nice way to save on my tax bill, the more devious among you may think, imagining large quantities of your personal wealth being stashed away in little Thomas's name, a sort of tax free hoard. Well of course that little wheeze doesn't work: the tax authorities stipulate that while it's appropriate for the grandparent to handle the money on the child's behalf, if it's withdrawn before the age limit, currently 16, there will be liabilities to back tax. After 16, young Thomas becomes personally responsible for the money. It's not yours any longer; it's Thomas's personal fortune. In other words, if you place the money in Thomas's name, think of it as no longer yours, it's gone, it's his to use later: full stop.

If that appeals to you, have a word with an advisor about matters such as the inheritance tax implications. Where and how to invest the money are other questions to consider. Grandparents often feel that since the money will be invested for someone else, not for them themselves, security is more important than the chance of large profits – with the accompanying chance of big losses.

The Trust Route

Another popular way is to set up a trust. One grandparent wrote:

> "We have set up a trust to be released when the older grand-child is 21."

Trusts are a technical area, where financial expertise is again needed. Some grandparent couples set up a trust to be established on the death of the first partner. This can have tax advantages, since it can reduce considerably the burden of inheritance tax which might be payable. Little Thomas benefits, since he's a beneficiary of the trust.

Why can't one of us, the surviving partner, be a beneficiary too, you may cry. In that way, the survivor can recover some of the money originally allocated to the trust. And the inheritance tax has been reduced. Good idea!

If only life were so simple. No, for that kind of trust, you're not allowed to become a beneficiary yourself. The trust can be worded to ask the trustees to pay particular care to the circumstances of the surviving partner, but that's not a legal obligation. In other words, you may be starving, while the hard-hearted trustees dispense large sums of the trust monies to Thomas and other beneficiaries, perhaps even that distant cousin you'd forgotten existed. You may grind your teeth, since no doubt you and your partner contributed to amassing the trust's wealth through your efforts during your lifetimes. But you're at the mercies of the trustees. Of course they're probably reasonable folk whom you and your partner trust implicitly. But it can be surprising how people change when put in charge of sums of money. So go and starve in a garret!

Another disadvantage is that Thomas can't have access to the cash until after the death of the first partner.

Other forms of trusts are also possible. A key decision for many trusts is the age at which you would like the grandchildren to have access to the trust monies. This is a matter where it's wise to talk things over with your children, so that there's agreement all round. Some grandparents, with their children's agreement, like to place the funds in trust until the grandchildren are in their thirties or older, but without necessarily either grandparent having died and so without inheritance tax necessarily being involved. Your children could be trustees, and the trustees could be given power to release money after the grandchildren reach an agreed age – perhaps 21 – but without prejudice to the grandchildren having full access after the age specified in the trust.

Setting up trusts is a matter for specialist guidance; once again, see a financial advisor about the pros and cons of the various methods possible.

Regular Contributions

> "My Grandad gives me £20 for Christmas and a tenner for my birthday." *Ellen, aged 11*

You can of course give a regular amount of money to your grandchild, perhaps every week or once a year, at your own discretion. Some grandparents feel it's more pleasant to see the grandchild's savings accumulate in this way, rather than investing a large one-off sum on his behalf. Money always gives pleasure to the recipient, even if it means missing the fun of opening presents: children remember generosity.

But there is a limit to the annual amount of money you can give to family members in this way, currently a few thousand pounds. Check with the taxman before you embark on this course.

The Child Trust Fund

Since 2005 the government has decided to help all young people when they face the costs of starting their careers, and has instituted the Child Trust Fund. The parents of every child born after September 2002 receive a £250 voucher, or £500 for families on tax credit. Another voucher is given when the child becomes seven years old. The parents can invest the vouchers in a fund for the child to use later. So how does this affect me, you ask?

Well, anyone – and that includes grandparents – can contribute up to £1,200 a year into the fund. And some grandparents find this a useful way of helping little Thomas get a good start in life. If this method appeals to you, do check the current limits: chancellors of the exchequer have a habit of making changes at budget times.

Risk and Reward

These are four of the more popular ways of putting funds aside for your grandchildren's future. If you decide you want to help, you need to think about where to invest your – little Thomas's – money. As with all investments, you trade risk for reward. More risky investments (e.g. shares) may be more rewarding (but may also lose more) than more secure ones. In making your decision, it's worth bearing in mind that it's often argued that in the longer term the stock market, for all its fluctuations, tends to outperform other investments, and investments for grandchildren are usually long term. But no one can be sure what the value of a stock market investment will be at the time little Thomas may need the money. If you want to be absolutely sure that little Thomas's investment doesn't lose value, you need to think of something like National Savings. But there are very many ways of investing for grandchildren that fall between these two extremes. If you want to help your grandchild in this way, just remember two things:

First, this is a complicated area, and it's wise – no, it's essential – to get financial advice over the many possibilities. Some routes are affected by time restrictions – limited to a set period of years before the full benefit of the financial package can be realised. In others the sum to be given to the grandchild is limited. Taxation arrangements change from time to time, which is another reason for getting specialist, up to date advice.

Second, what you do for one grandchild you'll want to do for all. And you don't know how many of the little darlings are going to come along. One grandfather wrote:

> "One of my close colleagues had four children, who between them produced 12 grandchildren. When they have their annual family gatherings, they have to book a whole guest house, since they're 22 altogether. I'd have difficulties just with names and birthdays. Gifts just don't bear thinking about!"

So do be careful. You don't want to find that what you've done for numbers 1-5 you can't afford to do for numbers 6-10. That way lies pain.

Supporting grandchildren in one way or another can give great pleasure. You're helping another family member take those important steps that otherwise might not have been taken. Whether you're appreciated or not doesn't matter. You've done this out of your love for the grandchildren, and you'll feel good about it. And what you do for them, in years to come they'll remember, and perhaps do the same for their own grandchildren too.

So, to summarise:

- Before making provision for your grandchild, make sure your own needs will be covered as far as possible.

- There can be tax advantages in helping your grandchild.

- Giving your grandchildren a nest egg, to help them to a good start in life, is one of the most rewarding actions a grandparent can take.

- Choose one of the ways that best appeals to you: give a lump sum, or establish a trust, or make a regular contribution, or use the Child Trust Fund, or other means.

- Remember that the investment with the best returns may also be the most risky.

- Be prudent: what you do for the first grandchild, you'll want to do for all the rest.

- Get advice, preferably from more than one good adviser, before deciding anything. And take your time about deciding.

CHAPTER 9

They're coming to Stay

Some of the many interesting things you can learn from small children:

- Bedrooms (especially next to yours) aren't the best places for keeping pet mice.

- Nor do bedrooms convert easily into forest dens.

- Plastic toys don't survive in hot ovens.

Yes, when they come to stay you might want to look in your oven before turning it on – one of the various extra precautions you might want to take when they're with you. But it's all worth it, you'll think when they go.

Having your grandchild to stay – one of the activities that grandmothers and grandfathers alike enjoyed enormously. At the same time, both felt that it needed some skill. One grandfather listed the following important skills:

- Effective burping.

- Persuading grandchild that broccoli purée is scrummy.

- Assuring grandchild that there are no horrible creatures under the bed.

Yes, they may seem humorous trivialities, but little problems loom large to little children.

So for a while, you're responsible for little James yourselves, you deal with the bath and bed routine, you can make sure that mealtimes are fun. And you haven't got the pressures of going off to work, so you can devote your time to your grandchild; you can relax together.

Having One Child to Stay

How old should grandchildren be before coming to stay with you on their own? We all know that little infants miss parents, and can be very upset by their absence. They need the security of the familiar face and familiar presence, so little ones will probably first stay at Gran's together with their parents. But as they become accustomed to Gran's place, there will come a time when it will be fun to have them by themselves.

It is their familiarity with you that largely determines when that should be. If they're used to calling in every day, they'll be able to stay with you quite early on. But if you live a long way away from the grandchildren, and see them rarely, don't rush it. Take it gradually. Let them come with their parents, and get used to your house while parents do the usual routine of meals and bed. Then perhaps give Mum and Dad an evening out, so that you can bed and bath little James, who's secure in the knowledge that Mum and Dad are returning later. Finally, when James agrees that it would be great to have a night just with Gran and Grandad, issue the invitation.

"Would you let us have James for a night?"

Note, just a night: don't hurry it. A homesick child won't be keen to come again.

This is the key: take it slowly. To use technical terminology, condition the experience so that your grandchild isn't faced with an unfamiliar situation, away from the security of home and Mum and Dad. You may think 'what a fuss over just having a loved grandchild to stay'. But it's well worth a little extra trouble to ensure that James enjoys the stay, and goes home wanting to come again.

And that raises a couple of other points that it's worth thinking about beforehand.

Make sure you know the routine that the grandchild usually follows. Can James bring a favourite bath toy? If there's a 'cuddly' of some sort that James can't bear to be parted from, do insist that 'cuddly' comes too, even if it's no more than a dirty old bit of cloth. Again, familiarity is important in establishing the security that young children need. Better find out James's favourite meals, something that he always enjoys helps to avoid any mealtime unhappiness. But be careful. One grandmother fed her grandchild so many of his favourite cheese potato cakes that he needed something for tummy pains afterwards. So familiarity even with the right children's medication might be useful too. Better make sure you've got some just in case James is unwell. Confirm whether you're up to speed with any allergies James might have, too.

It's essential to ask about boundaries; every family has rules about what's allowed and what's not allowed. Is bedtime flexible or not? Any rules about the TV and videos? Are friends allowed for sleepovers? Can James go swimming? Not only ensure you know the rules, but make sure that James knows that you know them too. That saves possible arguments.

Things to Do

Old, familiar routine is essential for a successful visit, but it's important to provide something new, something special too. What are you going to do with James? Sitting around hoping that those old toys you've had stored in the attic for 20 or 30 years will keep him happy for hours just won't do: modern toys are quite different. He's probably used to state of the art electronic playthings, equipped with all the latest bells and whistles.

Some of those old activities your children enjoyed are enjoyable still: unlike toys, they're timeless. Young children love threading beads to make patterns, learning to use scissors (not dangerous ones), making patterns out of paper, building with blocks, messing about with paints, messing with water, helping with the cooking/gardening ...unlike toys, these activities don't date.

Even so, ensure the grandchild brings a few of those personal toys that they love to play with at home. But perhaps he might also be allowed, as a special treat, to come with you to buy a new toy.

What are the outings that the grandchild enjoys at home – playing Pooh sticks, feeding ducks, playing in the park? Have a word with the parents and find out. At the same time, talk with parents in your locality who have children of the same age as your grandchild and note a few of the local facilities they suggest, not forgetting those suitable for wet days.

Walks are well known grandparent activities, offering plenty of opportunity for discussions on ecology and philosophy.

> "When grandparents take us for walks they always slow down past things like pretty leaves and caterpillars. They don't have to do anything except answer questions like 'why isn't God married?'"

If they're at the games stage, prepare a few pencil and paper games, or card games for an empty hour or so. (There's more about playtime in Chapter 11.) Invite children of similar ages in to play – nothing keeps children busier than playing with others of the same age. Then toys are often redundant as they make up their own games with the most bizarre objects: boxes become magic castles, logs become pirate ships, old clothes create weird characters. Imaginative games – there's nothing better.

Check the Telly schedules. It's tempting to sit James in front of

the screen, watching a suitable cartoon, knowing that, like nearly all children, he'll be fascinated for as long as you want to prepare the meal, or whatever. But make the box a last resort, or at
least restrict it – you don't want James going home and asking
Mum and Dad to put the box on every afternoon.

"Well, Grandma did."

"Did she now?"

Having More Than One Grandchild to Stay

Of course it's so much more fun with more than one grandchild;
having more than one child to stay can often be easier than having a single child. Two children can be company for each other,
can play together, and may need less attention. But not always:
brothers and sisters often quarrel, and the rivalry shown at home
can be reactivated away from home. That's where grannies and
grandpas with experience of working with little children, perhaps
in nurseries or first schools, come into their own. They're used to
handling small groups of young children.

If you think of having more than one grandchild, consider having
cousins, who don't see each other regularly. This can be an easier group to manage than siblings who are together every day. And
then there's a special pleasure in seeing young members of two
branches of your family enjoying each other's company under
your own roof.

If there aren't any cousins, perhaps James can bring a special
friend. And if you don't fancy putting up a second little visitor,
perhaps you know of a child of about James's age who could be
invited over for the day.

One grandfather wrote:

"There has been great satisfaction in having grandchildren to stay during school holidays so as to offer a part time alternative to the professional provision of childcare or organised holiday clubs. But it requires some skill, too."

Likes and Dislikes

Another grandfather raised an issue that must be familiar to all grandparents. Grandchildren are different, they all have different personalities, and some inevitably appear more lovable than others. How should one handle liking one grandchild much more than another?

Not an easy one. You're bound to have different feelings and attitudes to different grandchildren. Who hasn't heard a grandparent say something like "Oh I'm really fond of little X, she's such a *nice* child!," or "she's got such a *nice* nature", implying that little Y is not in great favour. Although your inner feelings will be different, try not to show them. The parents see every little goose as a swan: they're proud of each of their children, just as you are of yours. So when you see faults in the character of a grandchild, don't dwell on them, or worse, criticise or complain about the behaviour to the parents. Be positive: "Yes, he was a bit lively, but it was fun having him." And don't even think about the train drawn in red crayon over your newly painted cream hall.

Some grandparents manage to distinguish between the child and the behaviour. All grandchildren can be loved equally, and it's the behaviour, not the child that can be disliked. So try disapproving the behaviour, while reassuring the child that you still love him. And try not to compare the grandchildren.

Mind you, when little James is busy writing on your lounge walls in dayglo paints while Chloe, placid as ever, plays happily with the lego, it's not easy to remember these approaches. It's not easy to remember to distract James, to keep your temper, to disapprove strongly of the choice of canvas, rather than James. It's hard, in the moment of discovery, to think calmly of finding the biggest sheet of cardboard in the house and asking the little imp to draw you a picture on that.

It's a moment when it's so easy to compare Chloe and James, very much to James's detriment. "You stupid boy: your sister wouldn't do that!" Yes, it's so easy, but try not to do it. Your halo will almost be visible!

So, to summarise:

- Don't rush to have your grandchildren to stay: wait until they're fully familiar with you and your home.

- Find out their likes and preferences for food, games and routines beforehand.

- Find out the family rules about behaviour.

- Ensure they bring something they're fond of.

- But also provide something different.

- Having more than one child to stay is often easier than having one.

- Try to love all grandchildren equally: disapprove of the behaviour, not the child.

- Never compare one grandchild to the detriment of another.

- Most importantly, prepare.

CHAPTER 10

Handling Lively Grandchildren

First Child: "We just call our Granny 'Lou'. What do you call your Granny?"

Second Child: "Ours gets very stern. We call her 'The Gramminator'."

Behaviour, Discipline and Home Rules

It's a wonderful experience, looking after a little child again, and there were many of our grandparents who enthused about it. But even so, there were several grandparents who warned of possible snakes in paradise, 'handling naughty children who aren't your own', as one grandfather put it.

"I find keeping control difficult when they come to stay," one grandmother wrote. "Today, children seem so much less disciplined."

Yes, that's the old problem of differences between the generations. When they stay, whose discipline should they follow – home discipline, or Grandad's? As the anonymous grandmother wrote, modern home discipline is likely to be freer than yours was.

"But Mummy lets me leave the greens... stay down till midnight... go out in the rain... take what I want from the fridge..."

The little darling may be right; but they might be stretching the truth somewhat. Better check beforehand what the usual home rules are. Freedom is fine, but it shouldn't be license. One grandmother was very clear whose rules applied. When her four lively grandchildren came to stay she gathered them together and asked.

"Now whose house are you staying in?"
"Yours, Gran."
"And who's in charge in this house?"
"You are, Gran," they would chorus.
"Then we'll all remember that, and we'll all have fun."
"Yes, Gran."

And they did have fun, with little trouble and no arguments. Whenever a potential rebel tried a little challenge, she only had to ask "So who's in charge here?" and the mutineer deflated.

So do remember the old rule 'Start as you mean to go on'. And remember that 'no' never means 'maybe'. Once you fall into that trap, the children will be testing your resolve at every opportunity.

This is not an argument for enforcing a rigid system – far from it. Amanda, aged nine, when asked if there was anything she didn't like about being with her grandparents, wrote:

"I hate it when my Gran is cross with me for not tidying my room."

Amanda's parents probably had different standards of tidiness from Gran. Is it worth Gran trying to change Amanda's behaviour over the short period that she was visiting? And upsetting a loved grandchild? One child wrote:

"I just don't like getting slaps from my Gran."

Think about it. And perhaps bear in mind the wise words of another grandmother, who said:

"If you lose your temper with a child you are always the loser

– worse trouble follows. Make an effort to distract a child who's being difficult."

Telling off Harmlessly

Of course there are times when a wilful child won't be distracted, and your irritation mounts. You feel you have to stop that behaviour, whatever it may be; but you're not the parent, Harry isn't your child, he's your loved and normally lovable grandchild. What to do?

One thing *not* to do is to issue a threat that you can't or don't carry out:

> "If you jump on that chair once more Harry I won't take you out to the park this afternoon."

Not a good idea: you were taking little Jeanie with Harry, and you yourself want to visit the baker's on the way, so you're punishing others beside Harry. Moreover, the afternoon is a little way off, and you'll be tempted to forget the threat. But Harry won't, and so your next threat will be less effective.

If you're going to threaten, you must be able to carry it out, preferably immediately, so think carefully what you say.

Driving home, fed up with Harry's continually pinching little Katie, one exasperated grandmother said: "If you do that once more Harry, I'll stop the car and you'll have to get out and walk."

And Harry did pinch Katie again, and Gran did stop the car, ejected Harry, and did drive on. Of course it was a very safe road, she stopped after he'd walked a short distance on the pavement, and let him back in. A drastic threat, and not one to be recommended, but once made, it had to be carried out: and the pinching stopped.

Try rewarding the good behaviour, rather than punishing the

bad. When Harry repeatedly climbs all over your best chairs, in spite of your requests, wait for your opportunity, and try:

"Here's a juicy strawberry Harry. You've actually managed to sit still in that chair for a whole minute, instead of climbing all over it."

Don't call it bribery: we all like rewards for success, and Harry has to learn the difference between behaviour we approve of, behaviour we don't mind, and behaviour we won't accept. Rewards are usually more effective than punishment for successful learning.

Some grandparents tease the child out of bad behaviour by issuing threats that are so obviously fantastic that the child can't help being distracted by them. One grandfather used this technique, saying: "If you do that again Harry, I'll spiflicate you."

"You'll *what* Grandad?"

Grandad looks stern and very serious. "I said I'll spiflicate you."

Harry is intrigued, unsure, and slightly anxious. "What's spiflicate then, Grandad?"

"I'm not going to tell you Harry. But you'll find out, and you won't like it one little bit. The last little boy I spiflicated cried for hours."

Harry is getting worried. "So tell me what you did, Grandad."

Grandad raises a warning finger. "I won't, Harry; spiflicating is too horrible to describe. So you'd better stop climbing over that chair and sit down quietly."

Even the most lovable of grandchildren sometimes has to be brought into line. Try several different approaches, but do remember that the ultimate authority is that of the parents, not you. It's always wise to discuss with the parents what are the sanctions that they accept. And hopefully they'll be rarely needed.

Off on Their Own

But behaviour isn't only a question of discipline. How far do you let the grandchildren manage their activities on their own? Again this depends very much on age, obviously. But when they're older, should you allow them to go to the local swimming pool with a friend? Can they ride their bikes down to the local playground? Should you let them go out for a walk and take a picnic? Activities such as these pose possible dangers: they're not your children, but they're in your care, and the parents aren't about.

Do discuss issues like these with the parents beforehand. It's important to clear the ground as far as responsibility is concerned. If something you haven't covered crops up, it's always best to ring the parents to get the yea or nay, even if it means deferring the activity till the next day, or even missing it.

But don't be dissuaded from having the grandchild or grandchildren to stay by thinking about possible unhappy events. If we did that all the time, what a lot of fun we'd miss. Enjoy little Harry's visits to you. Grandchildren only want to come for a very short time: the golden years soon pass, and you must make the most of them.

Once again, do talk matters over with the parents first, and try to agree a few ground rules. It shouldn't be difficult – after all one of the parents will be very used to your dos and don'ts.

So, to summarise:

● Make allowances for modern views on discipline; they're probably different from your own.

● Check with the parents before setting ground rules when you're in charge.

● And discuss with the parents what sanctions are acceptable.

● Having set ground rules, tell the children, and then stick to them.

● Being firm doesn't mean being strict, though 'no' should never mean 'maybe'.

● Threats and punishments for bad behaviour are not as effective as rewarding good behaviour.

● Don't lose your temper, and certainly don't slap.

● Finally, "Govern a family as you would cook a small fish: very gently." (Chinese proverb)

CHAPTER 11

Playtime

"I like best playing dominoes with my Nana and footie with my Grandad."

Playing with the grandchildren: a time when grandfathers really come into their own. Yes, grandmothers enjoyed playing with the grandchildren, but for grandfathers it was one of the activities they enjoyed most of all. One grandfather remembered meeting his baby grandson, 10 months old, for the first time. Soon Grandad was on his hands and knees, crawling round the furniture, playing hide and seek. As the baby squealed with delight, the baby's father said admiringly: "Ah the old tricks haven't been forgotten!" And Grandad still recalls the little surge of pleasure that gave him.

The games grandparents play are endless, and this isn't the place to attempt to catalogue them. You may think that hide and seek round the furniture won't last long, and you're right; it's fun with babies, but babyhood doesn't last long. Yet children of all ages enjoy hide and seek in different settings. Play it when you're out for a walk, play it in the garden, play it in the house – old favourites are fun. You haven't even got to find a good hiding place: for young children the fun is in finding the hider, so concealing yourself – very inadequately – behind a lamp-post, allowing yourself to be spotted and found – that's great fun for little ones.

Grandmother's footsteps is an appropriately titled game for this book, but be careful. It's an example of a game which can lead to disputes, fiercely argued with all the righteousness of true believers.

"Sophie, I saw you move: I'm afraid you're out."

"I wasn't moving Grandma: I'd stopped when you turned and looked."

"No, Sophie, I definitely saw you."

"No Grandma, you couldn't have"......and so on.

Nothing Succeeds Like Success

Ball games are always popular. Many children said how much they enjoyed playing football and rugby with their Grandads, and cricket on the beach was another favourite. Grandfathers enjoy rediscovering old skills (but be careful – the old knees and ankles aren't as flexible as they once were), and grandmothers can allow budding Beckhams to score goals at will – almost.

But one or two boys said they didn't like it when Grandad always won. Of course children have to learn that there are others better than they are. But children must be allowed to win tackles and score goals, if only to enter later challenges in the knowledge that they *can* win. There's nothing like success for breeding confidence. And don't forget praise: praise – and lots of it – is another very important ingredient that grandparents can offer. It helps to build the self-esteem of a diffident child.

One grandmother said: "I do enjoy having races with my little grandchildren, and letting them win at the last minute."

Time, the Key Ingredient

Repetition is a feature that little children enjoy. Grandparents spend hours at the local children's playground, pushing children on the swings, and catching them on the slides, over and over again. Willingly telling them the same old story time after time, or playing the same card game for what seems like hours. One 10 year old put it succinctly: "I like going to my gran's. She always has TIME." (sic)

And that's the vital ingredient that grandparents can offer: time. Time for card games like snap, time for board games like snakes and ladders – and time to make pretend mistakes, going up the snakes and down the ladders, to give the child the pleasure of correcting a grown-up: "silly Grandpa!" Time too for all the familiar childhood activities that had to be restricted to weekends and holidays when your own children were young. And when the grandchildren are older, time for meeting requests like: "Come fishing, Grandad," and you daren't say no...

Meanwhile, for younger children, don't forget the illicit pleasure that sharing a secret offers. Whispering something into Lucy's ear that no one else but you and she knows – oh the hidden delight! And especially if it's a secret that's kept from the parents. For once Lucy feels she knows something Mummy and Daddy don't, and that confers an enjoyable sense of power. Short lived of course, but wonderfully exhilarating while it lasts.

Indoor Games

There's no problem about indoor games when you visit your grandchildren; their house is probably full of children's games. But when they visit you, it's well worth keeping a small box of games that they enjoy, preferably something different from those that they're familiar with at home. Many of those that you used to play with your children may well be battered, pieces lost, counters missing, or just plain out of date. So invest in some new ones. Not too many, just a few that they know are special to Grandad & Grandma.

Not all old games should be discarded. It's strange, but those that involve activity seem to appeal across the generations. Any construction activity, like a box of lego, or even an ancient meccano set, is usually a winner. Indoor games of skill, like that old miniature snooker set (but under supervision at first – watch those cues) is fine for older children, but younger ones may find it frustrating. One grandfather kept an old bagatelle game specially for the grandchildren's visits. They looked forward to playing bagatelle as much as seeing grandpa – and so did the parents.

The snooker illustration makes another point. Do try to play games suitable for little Jack. To take an extreme example, he might enjoy playing snap when he's four, but he certainly won't enjoy scrabble. If Jack starts to get cross, he may well be finding the game too hard, so change it. Playtime should be fun.

Keep their toys and games in a place they know and that's convenient for them. Then when they arrive they can find them, and bring out whatever they choose. The contents will change according to the age of the grandchildren, but some games fascinate most ages. And it's worth having a designated place where they know they can play, on a particular floor or a specially covered table – particularly if they want to paint or draw.

Happy grandchildren playing quietly bring contentment. But be particularly wary when all is too quiet. One pair of grandparents decided to sell their leather three piece suite. When the prospective purchaser pulled out the settee, tattooed right across the back was the name of one of the grandchildren. Too late, they recalled that unexpectedly peaceful hour, a couple of days earlier, when Jack had been given a compass and shown how to draw circles. He'd actually spent a very happy time, ensconced quietly behind the settee, using the compass point to prick out his name in the leather.

Older grandparents may remember Uncle Mac, on the old Children's Hour, signing off the programme with: "Be good, but not so good that someone says 'now then, and what have you been up to?'." It never pays to relax and enjoy the peace when all is quiet on the grandchildren front.

Outdoor Play

The weather's fine, the sun has his hat on, the great outdoors beckons. What to do with the grandchildren? They know what they like to do. Ball games, as mentioned earlier, are great favourites.

"I like playing cricket, football and rugby with my grandparents."

No one needs a full team to play family team games. Even just two a side touch rugby, (grandparents against grandchildren? – you haven't really got to run) is fun. French cricket needn't involve more than a bowler and a batsman, or woman, but you'll need a setting where balls – tennis balls, preferably – can be easily retrieved. Yes, eight year olds are energetic little creatures. But your sporting days with them won't last long: by the time they're into their teens their improving skills will probably have long surpassed your declining ones (unless you're a great sportsman or woman).

If you live by the sea, there's never any problem with outdoor activities. Find a beach, and grandchildren are happy all day. Skipstones competitions, sandcastle building, kite flying, frisbee floating – even just splashing about in the water. Do remember that little ones burn up energy quickly and need frequent refuelling. Take plenty of food and drink, and be prepared for any little accidents with the younger ones.

Older ones will want more swimming, and may be quite sophisticated over dress. Be prepared for juvenile embarrassment when they have to appear with you in your old beach shorts and swimwear.

"Where did you get those shorts, Grandad – in the war?"

Take it all in good part. Finding time to play with your grandchildren will bring immense rewards.

So, to summarise:

- Always make time to play.

- Don't win every time; let the children win frequently.

- Don't choose games that you enjoy, but which are too hard for the children.

- Keep an easily accessible box of games ready for them.

- Try playing a few of your old favourite games.

- But also invest in some new ones.

- Be suspicious when they're unusually quiet.

CHAPTER 12

Watching Them Develop

"A child's mind is not a vessel to be filled, but a fire to be kindled."

The phone rings: your children are excited: "Mum, we just have to tell you. Daniel took his first step today!"

"Isn't that great dear! Now you're going to be busy. And when you bring him over next I'll have to be really careful with those saucepan handles on the cooker. He'll be able to reach them."

So as well as joining in the celebrations, you might as well slip in a word or two about the new hazards that Daniel might encounter now that he's above floor level.

Milestones

Watching the grandchildren develop gave more pleasure to grandfathers than any other aspect of having grandchildren, and for grandmothers it came next only to holding the first grandchild. To observe the first smiles of recognition, to hear the first words, to see the first faltering steps – all those milestones of childhood that you recall from your own child-rearing days – these afford great pleasure.

Many parents like to share these moments with the grandparents. It's not always easy for them to enjoy the moment with other parents – comparisons can bring unhappy feelings and possible worries to one of the parties. But you don't have any little children, and since you're 'family', the parents can share their pleasure at Daniel's progress with you: even boast a little about it. And you can encourage them to think what a little boy wonder they're raising.

During these stages some parents will raise Daniel's progress – or apparent lack of it – with the grandparents in order to seek reassurance, rather than to share pride. You've been through these stages before, so you can advise, they think. They'll have the latest baby advice book, but still there's nobody like their own parents for discussing their concerns about the baby's development.

"I'm a bit worried about his talking, Mum. You remember Barbara, who had her baby the same time as me. Well her Horace is like Daniel, 13 months – actually a week younger than Daniel – and he knows all sorts of words. She was telling me that Horace can say 'Mummy', and 'Daddy', and point to the light when she asks him to. Daniel can't do any of these. You don't think he's going to be slow, Mum?"

Time for you to recall all those infants you knew who didn't talk until they were 15 months, 18 months, nearly two years old, and ended up with first class degrees at Oxford or Cambridge. Time to remember what Dr Spock used to say about the age of starting to talk, time to ask what the health visitor or the baby clinic has said, and time to echo the reassurance they've given and that the parents need. And when six months later they ring to tell you what a wonderful vocabulary Daniel has, just enjoy and share their pleasure.

Recording Progress

Of course you'll want some record of Daniel's development. Those framed photos that they sent you as birthday or Christmas presents are nice mantelpiece decorations, but you'll want more than that. The parents themselves will be keeping a more detailed record of Daniel's childhood, and you'd like one for yourselves.

Your record will be slightly different, since you'll want to include those shots of Daniel with you yourself, at your house, on holiday with you – something just a little more personal to you, perhaps.

Prepare by acquiring an album for photographs. It's never too early to get one, since you don't want to lose those very early shots of Daniel's first few weeks. Or if you're into digital photography, think of how you're going to organise those discs or store those images.

Videos? Sound recordings? There are so many ways in which memories can be recorded, memories which in years to come Daniel himself will find great fun to re-live disbelievingly ("Was that really me in the bathtub, Gran?"), and later perhaps show to his own children.

Some enthusiastic grandparents like to make a scrapbook of their grandchild's early development. Clearly this isn't going to be easy if you're one of those grandparents whose grandchildren live a long way away. But it's always possible to make a little memento, a miniature scrapbook, perhaps covering a holiday together, something you'll enjoy browsing through later.

It's interesting to record Daniel passing the common milestones of smiling, crawling, standing, walking, talking and so on, but even more interesting to watch his personality and intellect develop. Going to school, getting the first report from school on his behaviour and progress, these are all events that proud parents like to share with you. Does he show any of the characteristics of your children, you wonder. Or even of his grandparents – especially those likeable traits, those scholastic abilities, those sports skills…

Of course, Daniel may bring home a poor report that you're asked to see. Don't get angry about it. There's the story of the 13 year old being berated by his parent for a very poor school report, who suddenly asked "Do you think it's my heredity or my environment, Dad?"

Rewarding Progress

The pleasure and excitement at a good report belong initially to Daniel, and then his parents. But grandparents have a part to play too. At the very least, give praise where you can. In addition, a reward for a good school report is often something for grandparents to offer. But be careful: if you've more than one grandchild, they won't all have equally good reports, and you don't want to make the other grandchildren too envious. Look at the reports on Daniel's brothers and sisters too, and remember that improvement, hard won, is just as deserving of reward as high achievement, effortlessly reached: some would say more so. It's rare to find a report with nothing to commend, and there are always ways of finding good points on it.

Of course you might want to pause before putting your hand in your pocket. 'If I do this now, will Daniel expect it for every report', you may well think. Will he and his little brothers and sisters come running up at the end of every term, waving a report and expecting a handout? Perhaps you're one of these impulsive grandparents whose natural generosity overrides considerations like these. Whatever you decide, remember to give plenty of praise where it's due.

Do treat the grandchildren as fairly as possible. But remember that while equality is an important principle to follow, no principle is completely inflexible, and just occasionally you might want to vary it.

You Have a Part to Play

It's during this time of development that grandparents can exercise important influences on their grandchildren. One grandfather wrote that what gave him most satisfaction was imparting skills to his grandchildren, giving them new abilities that might stay with them throughout their lifetime. These can be simple skills, perhaps teaching five year olds how to tie bows in shoelaces, or more advanced skills, like teaching fly-fishing to 12 year olds.

Young children are interested in almost everything. The primary school years are the time in which they are eager to learn, so seize the opportunity to enlarge your grandchildrens' horizons. If Daniel shows an interest in your hobby, you'll get great pleasure at seeing him share your enthusiasm for it. And you must reciprocate, too. Maybe football isn't one of your likes, but you'll have to spend time on the touchline when Daniel is playing for the school second team in the under 12 schools league, even if it's pouring with rain and starting to sleet. And if you can remember who won the 2006 World Cup, and by how much, you'll gain brownie points.

As the grandchildren develop, so they gradually grow away from you. It's no reflection on you – it happens to parents and grandparents alike. By the time they're into adolescence they'll be listening to their friends and to other adults, as much if not more than their family. But if you've used that special grandparent relationship with them, taken part in their development, helped them grow up, you'll have enjoyed a great privilege. Then when they themselves become responsible adults with families of their own, they'll make sure that the new generation will be as involved with you as they were themselves.

So, to summarise:

● Share parents' concerns about milestones, and reassure where possible.

● Make a record of your grandchild's development, and think how you'll want to store the memories you'll gather.

● Be interested in their school reports.

● Reward them for effort, as well as success.

● Teach them some of the skills you possess.

● Share in their own enthusiasms, too.

CHAPTER 13

Helping language develop

"A novice is a nun in a monastery."

"Socrates died of an overdose of wedlock."

"Henry the Eighth had difficulty walking because he had an abbess on his knee."

Words, word, words! Watching your grandchildren's language develop is a particular pleasure. And language is such an important skill; communicating confidently is *the* key ability, central to getting on in school and life. We grandparents can help the grandchildren improve their language in so many ways. The more we talk with them, the more we read with them, write to them – all this helps their use of good language, and helps avoid some of the schoolboy howlers mentioned above. Here are a few of the more important ways in which we can help.

Rhymetime

When they're little, they'll enjoy those nursery rhymes that you've almost forgotten. If you read the rhymes to them they'll soon pick them up, and then they'll really enjoy the game of filling in the words you omit, or hesitate over. And if you occasionally put in a wrong word, in order to see if you can catch them out, they'll have great fun correcting you.

"No Gran! Jack and Jill went up the hill, not the stairs: don't be silly!"

And playing with rhymes, even at a very early age, will help with that central skill of learning to read.

A book of nursery rhymes is a good investment. The old one you used to have has probably been lost long ago. Buy a new one, with attractive pictures accompanying the rhymes, pictures that attract Ellie's attention. You'll soon learn the rhymes again, and you'll be able to repeat them when the book itself isn't available – on a journey, away from home and so on.

Storytime

Then as they get older, "Tell me a story, Grandad."

Grandparents have time to tell all those stories that children enjoy. Children remember the stories you tell them, and the old ones are so often the favourites. One child remembered: "My grandma used to tell me stories about the three little pigs, and one about Goldilocks and the three bears."

And one grandfather wrote:

"Something I particularly enjoyed was making up and telling bedtime stories to grandchildren. There's something special about creating something unique for kids (and family). By the same token I enjoyed creating/making forts, dolls houses, farms, garages, dens..."

Better hone your story telling skills, Grandad. You're going to be in demand at bedtime for a few years. Can you make up stories about an imaginary figure, a figure who appears and reappears in the stories you tell? If you can, so much the better.

Many grandparents use their own imagination to produce a story that's appealing to their listeners. But some vary this by asking the children to contribute their own imaginative ideas. For example:

"One day, Freddie Frog decided to go for a ride on his magic ... magic what do you think, Ellie?"

"His magic…er.. cheese, Grandad."

"Right: so Freddie jumped on his magic cheese, said the magic word, and off they went up into the sky, until, far below they saw a … a what, Ellie?"

This gives Ellie a chance to use her own imagination, as well as giving her a sense of ownership of the story. It's the forerunner of creative writing. So encourage your little grandchild to play with words and stories; who knows, you may be fostering the talents of the next J.K.Rowling.

But if telling imaginative stories isn't a skill you possess, reading an existing story, one Ellie chooses herself, is the next best thing. But none of this missing out the odd page or paragraph so as to finish and return downstairs to Match of the Day. That's a subterfuge that any four year old will spot at once. She'll soon know every sentence, every word, and you won't be allowed to get away with anything. So don't try!

Family stories

When they're a little older, they'll really enjoy hearing stories about their mother or father when they were little.

"Tell me about the time when Mummy fell into the duck pond, Grandad." Or better: "Tell me about the time that Daddy was naughty and ran away in the shop." There's nothing like a tale of one's naughty parents to give pleasure to little children.

One particular side to story telling is the chance to draw out of memory those bits of family history that you alone may possess, bits of oral history handed down to you by an earlier generation. These are part of the rich fabric of family culture that new members of the family love to hear and to store away, much as you did yourself. Parents don't have the time to pass many of these tales on to the children: it often seems to be the grandparents who hold the keys to our past, and who can unlock the doors to a treasure house of tales for the grandchildren to enjoy.

Any story about family members interests the young, whether the characters are present or long past. And the more scurrilous, usually the better. And don't forget your own escapades, too.

"Did you really swim naked... scrump apples... run away from school Grandad! Gosh, I wish I'd got to know you sooner!"

Stories about the grandchildren themselves always fascinate, too. One 11 year old wrote:

> "I like it when my Nana tells us stories about when we were young and did funny things."

It's all too easy to forget that our own story often fascinates the young. We remember events that happened half a century or more ago as if they happened yesterday. Yet to the young, they're distant history. Think of the time 50 years or more before your own birth: that seems pretty ancient. Well that's how your own early years seem to the grandchildren. To them, you're a survivor, a period piece, with a story to tell. And don't hesitate to tell the story. When they ask "what did you do in the war, Grandad?" think back to those days of shortages and of chocolate rationing, to the sound of air raid sirens, the smell of the shelters, the shake of enemy bombs, the sight of squadrons of daylight raiders forming up over England...and tell them.

Before my mother died, she wrote the story of her early years, growing up in a mining family in the South Wales coalfield, and the disappointments and the successes the family experienced. Her grandchildren were enthralled; they read it eagerly. Quite apart from the family characters they had never met, the daily life – baths in the kitchen, the milkman driving up in a pony and trap, school classes of 50 pupils or more – the different tapestry of long ago daily life amazed them.

So think of writing down a few memories of your own childhood. Your grandchildren will cherish them, and – who knows – might later write their own experiences of growing up in the twenty-first century, something to add to a developing family history.

Help with Schoolwork

When they're older, they may well turn to you for help over long forgotten school subjects, perhaps with some homework or holiday task. Some subjects – perhaps algebra? – you might well recall with some pain. Should you help?

If it's a simple factual question, perhaps some information needed for an essay, of course you should. It's easier just to ask Gran or Grandad when World War Two started, than to go to the internet to find out. But when it's a call for assistance with more complicated activities, be careful. Remember that teaching approaches have changed since your day. It's generally wiser not to try to introduce Ellie to methods of learning you remember from 50 or more years ago; that way lies confusion. Unless you're sure of what you're doing, and are familiar with the methods used in Ellie's class, better leave it to teacher.

But long before your grandchildren get to this stage, they have to learn to read.

Getting book-borne

You're sure to be in demand when little Ellie starts to read. You'll be wanted to help over the hard words, to encourage and praise. Perhaps there'll be reading homework that you'll have to certify that she has read, and perhaps you'll have to write some comments for teacher on her performance.

Reading is such an important skill for children to acquire: it's the basis of education, whether it's education through reading books, or via the classroom whiteboard, or computer screen. (The blackboard has long since disappeared, Grandad.) So seize every chance to help the grandchildren read.

If the book is on the hard side, better to read along with Ellie, perhaps a sentence each in turn, rather than let her struggle alone. And if she flounders over a word, don't hesitate to help and encourage her: reading should be fun, not a struggle.

Even if your grandchild lives a long way away, it's still possible to help with reading. One grandmother kept in touch by reading a book over the phone. Every night she would read the next few pages. Later, as the grandchild's reading skills improved, they took it in turns to read a chapter to each other, and as the years passed, she enjoyed seeing his vocabulary grow and his literary horizons enlarge: more importantly it forged a wonderful bond between the two. The phone bills rose, but as she said, a grandson's love is worth so much more than any phone bill.

Make the most of this time, for it may well be the last chance you'll have of helping with serious stuff. Once Ellie's away and book-borne, she'll prefer to read a favourite book by herself.

So, to summarise:

- Buy a book of nursery rhymes and enjoy them together.

- Make up imaginative stories, as well as telling old favourites.

- Don't forget family stories, especially any about their own parents' childhood.

- And also stories of the grandchildren themselves when they were younger.

- Help and encourage with reading; don't criticise.

- Don't be disappointed if they don't read as quickly as you expect: it's not an easy skill to acquire.

● Don't interfere with the school's teaching methods.

● Finally, seize every chance to talk, read and write with your grandchildren.

CHAPTER 14

Giving Presents

"I used to like going for walks with my Nana when I was younger. She used to give me sweets. But now she always gives me money. For Christmas and my birthday she gives me more money and lots of presents."

Remembering

Giving presents is an art. Let's begin by stressing the first rule: don't forget! There's no problem over remembering Christmas, but little William and the rest of his tribe will expect presents on their birthdays, and you'll be upset if you suddenly notice that the birthday has gone, and you've missed it. Not just upset, you'll be devastated: what did William think when he opened his presents and there wasn't one from us, you'll agonise. Don't disappoint them.

So do invest in a birthday book, and enter the birthday dates in it. When you enter the dates, insert the year of birth too. That's an easy way of always getting the right age on the birthday card. You don't want a 'thank you' letter from William reminding you that "I'm actually 10, not nine, Gran."

If you're someone who's likely to forget to consult the birthday book, then transfer the dates each year from birthday book to the daily diary. Some people do that when they change their diaries, each New Year.

If you've got a big tribe of grandchildren and a small memory it may be worthwhile making a note of the presents you give. That way you won't make the mistake of giving William the same present as his older brother had last year. That's not a good move. Worse still is giving William the same present as you gave William himself last year – that's definitely a no-no, and a reminder in your birthday book will help you to avoid it.

Money or Presents

The next point is that choosing a suitable gift is an art that's needed only for a relatively short period in a child's life. By the time children reach the age of eight or nine they'll usually prefer cash, so that they can choose their own present. Perhaps they're saving up for a big purchase, and would like a contribution towards the latest state-of-the-art phone with camera and TV, that every other little multimillionaire in year three is reported to own. So money is what the little capitalists want then. I believe there are some grandparents who specify what the money should or should not be used for ('A birthday present of £40 providing it's spent on a set of books for school, and not spent on a set of X rated videos.') But most grandparents are far too wise to go down that road, and leave matters to the family.

Do be careful over fairness if you're giving money. Children do compare presents, and you don't want little William wondering why you only gave him £20 for his birthday, while his brother had £25 for his. So do treat them equally, or if there are reasons why you don't, explain them. ("You'll have £25 when you're as old as your brother, William.")

But what about those first few years when the grandchildren aren't yet able to handle money sensibly, and look forward eagerly to a surprise present from Gran and Grandad. What should you give them?

The rule here is to consult with the parents. They'll know what the children are into, so they'll be sure to suggest something that will be appreciated, and not linger in the back of the toy cupboard, perhaps never to be used. One grandmother wrote:

"Always consult with the parents before buying presents, especially major presents. Don't buy presents to suit you, but think of the grandchildren and what they need."

Moreover, consulting with the parents often avoids that dreaded duplication of presents and the cry of "Oh I've got that already from Uncle Sebastian." Mum and Dad probably have a shrewd idea of what else is in the post for William, and can alert you to what little William would appreciate.

Sometimes it's relatively easy. "Oh a jigsaw, please," Mum says. So off you go to be bewildered by a vast selection of jigsaws at the local toyshop.

Many toys and games give suggested age ranges on the packaging, so look at this before buying. But remember that manufacturers naturally tend to be optimistic, so use your common sense too. Perhaps William is advanced for his age so, as Chapter 11 stressed, make due allowances for your knowledge of William's development. And think too about the theme of the jigsaw. William is unlikely to be enthused about a jigsaw that builds into a fairy princess if he's keen on racing cars. So think about your grandchild's interests when you're making your choice.

Later, choices may become harder. You may think you know what would please William, but you may be wrong. So again, have a word with the parents. They'll know better than you what would please William. You may be thinking how much William enjoyed playing with that train set when you last saw him, and so you were about to buy an extension set of extra rails and carriages. "Forget it Grandad," Mum says. "He's into a bloodthirsty phase, collecting man eating robots now. Why not get him the Bonecrusher Monster – he's missing that one." So you take their advice, pop in an extra couple of pygmies for the Bone-crusher to work on, and William is delighted.

Overseas Presents

Grandchildren who live overseas add another dimension to present giving. The cost of sending a bulky parcel to Australia may well be greater than the cost of the present itself. And it may not be easy to pack the present so that it arrives in an undamaged condition. Opening a birthday present to find an irreparably damaged toy obviously causes a lot of disappointment.

There are ways round this. Some grandparents order presents through firms that offer to deliver internationally. A reputable firm will ensure that the packing is much safer than any you can provide, and will deal with the boring little formalities of customs declarations at the same time.

Alternatively – and this is the more popular way – transfer to your son or daughter enough money to cover presents for the next few years, and ask them to open a 'present account'. Then when birthdays approach, ask son or daughter to buy a present from Gran and Grandad, and to withdraw a suitable sum from the account to cover it. That way you can be sure that the present obtained on your behalf will be one that William will be pleased to have, and will be delivered safely too.

You can arrange matters so that you yourselves have access to the account as well as son or daughter. The advantage of this is that if and when you go to visit the overseas family, there's cash already there in an account that you can draw on yourselves.

We've been discussing big presents. But don't forget the little presents that grandparents enjoy giving too.

> "I like going to my Gran's because she gives me sweets every time I go there." *Olivia, aged 8*

Maybe the few sweets seem a trivial gift. But sometimes the regularity of the trivial gifts constitutes a small secret between gran and grandchild, and cement a relationship that will last, and provide a happy, comforting warmth in years to come.

And present giving can be infectious. What's nicer for us grandparents than to open an envelope on our birthdays, and to find a primitive picture, accompanied by those little words "with love to Gran/Grandad"? The drawing may be primitive, the writing immature and the paper grubby, but doesn't the tiny present please you?

Don't forget the 'Ho-hos'. Ho-hos are those unexpected presents, bought on the spur of the moment and given out of the blue. ("I saw this magazine had an issue on international rugby stars/rock bands/or whatever, and thought you might like it.") I've no idea why they're called ho-hos; perhaps it's an association with Father Christmas and his Ho-ho-ho. Whatever the reason, a surprise gift, a ho-ho, may provide as much pleasure and enjoyment as the expected large birthday or Christmas present.

So, to summarise:

- Keep a record of your grandchildren's birthdays and year of birth.
- Always consult with the parents before buying a present.
- Use manufacturers' suggested age ranges as a guide only.
- Treat your grandchildren equally.
- Don't send expensive presents overseas: use a local bank account.
- Unexpected 'Ho-hos' can give much pleasure.

CHAPTER 15

Long-distance Grandparenting

A little boy was asked where his grandparents lived:

"Oh, they live at the airport. When we want them to come we fetch them, and when it's time for them to go home we take them back to the airport."

Today, many children live and work far away from their parents, and keeping in touch isn't always very easy. When the grandchildren arrive and you feel the need to be close to them during their growing up, how best to do this?

Keeping in Touch by Phone

You give the young parents a ring one afternoon. The phone lifts off its cradle, but no one says anything; all is silence. For a moment you're puzzled, but then the penny drops. "James," you ask, "is that you?" No answer. "It's Gran here, James."

Still no answer, and then a little chuckle and the sound of the phone being dropped and the approaching footsteps of one of the parents.

When families live at a distance, and you see your grandchildren infrequently, talking with them over the phone gives grandparents much pleasure. It's a sign of the grandchildren's growing independence, and the fostering of a direct, personal relationship between the two of you. As James becomes familiar with the phone, the parents may want to encourage him to use it to talk to you.

"Come and speak to Grandad, James."

"Hello, Grandad."

"Hello, James." Silence. "What have you been up to today?"

"Playing."

"What were you playing, James?"

Silence, or maybe "Games."

The art of conversation is something children have to learn, and we can help them a little. Conversations with young children are often liable to fade into monosyllables, and that's particularly true for conversations over the phone. It takes a while for them to get used to the idea that it really is Grandad or Grandma speaking out of that little toy thing called a phone or a mobile. After all, there's no one there.

Parents have little need to talk to their young children over the phone – they're with them most of the 24 hours in the day. Grandparents, on the other hand, do love phone conversations with the grandchildren. This is especially true for distant grandparents, of course. So let's be ready for the phone call.

If James is likely to be on the end of the line, prepare a few topics that you know he'll enjoy hearing about. If he's not able to ask good questions yet, at least he'll like to listen to what your puppy's been up to, or to the tale of the naughty girl who stole your milk, or whatever. If James enjoys one side of a conversation, he'll be more likely to develop a good two way conversational style with you when he's a little older, and that will give you pleasure too.

Of course you want to encourage James to offer a little back, to say something to you. Young children often find it easier to respond to something that requires a factual answer, rather than having to describe something off their own bats, a principle that applies to face to face conversations too, but is perhaps more important over the phone. And offering a few alternatives, so that he gets the hang of how to answer, also helps.

"I wonder what you were playing, James. Was it hide-and-seek?"
"No."
"No? Was it spacemen?"
"No? So what was it?"

...and as well as achieving at least a few 'nos', you may well get James to volunteer that he was playing on the trampoline or whatever, giving you the opportunity to draw out some information about it.

When you ring to keep in touch with your family, it's usually one of the parents who answers when the grandchildren are young. Then after you've had your chat, the grandchild can be asked to come and talk.

"Come and say hello to Grandad, James."

Then you try to have your little chat with James. James of course might not have appreciated being dragged away from his game of dinosaurs just because Mum has happened to finish her conversation with you. For that reason, it may not be a productive chat. So ask the parents when would be a good time to talk to the busy little chap, and do have something interesting to tell him.

It's good to phone and ask to speak to James himself, not just as one of the family. Of course you do that on his birthday – remembering that you don't want to ring at a time when the conjurer he's asked for is in the middle of entertaining him and his friends.

Do it on other occasions too. A call specially for him helps to keep that bond between you bright and polished.

Later still, when your teenage grandchildren have mobile phones permanently attached to their ears, you may think back wryly to those happy days when you helped them develop a conversational style. But by then they'll be too busy texting and chatting with their contemporaries to bother with Grandad.

Keeping in Touch by Post

Some time after you've started telephone conversations, you'll begin to get written communications. Parents proudly send you a sheet of paper with an indecipherable squiggle.

"It's James's drawing of you, Grandad!"

Later you get a piece of paper with James's first attempt at his name. It's hard to recognise, but you can just make out the shapes of one or two letters. Later still you'll get something recognisable as a letter – perhaps a sentence or two. Or maybe you'll get a card from a holiday spot, with "To Grandad, Love from James." written on it.

Do reply. To encourage the writing habit, send something in return – your grandchildren will love to receive something through the post, addressed to them. A card with a picture is always a good bet, and so easy to send, but anything is better than nothing. No one wants to send something into the blue without a response – that kills any thoughts of sending again. But knowing that a reply will always come – that's an encouragement. And don't always wait to hear from grandchildren before writing to them. The occasional card from you will give great pleasure, even if they're not as conscientious as you about keeping in touch.

Communicating by Computer

The same principle applies to newer means of communication – e-mails for example, as was mentioned in Chapter 3. Grandchildren become computer literate very early these days, and well capable of e-mailing letters and photos. Many have e-mail addresses of their own.

Better take the plunge and get enrolled on that computer course you've been thinking about. Having grandchildren is the best of reasons for it. You'll soon be competent at these new communication techniques, and don't forget, you have the time to hone those skills. Why, before long you'll be advocating broadband, persuading your children to download an internet telephony programme, to install a webcam...

Communication Problems

So far we've assumed that grandparents and children use the same language. Not always true: there are many ethnic minority families where a grandparent, often living with the family, has little English, whereas the grandchildren use English as their first language. The parents, the middle generation, who can usually manage both English and the other language often act as rough and ready interpreters. But there's no denying that in this situation, much is lost. The grandparents in particular feel sadness at their inability to pass on stories about the family, a point mentioned in Chapter 6. They regret that their grandchildren will not know enough of the life and culture they themselves experienced as children, growing up in a distant land.

This situation, lack of communication between grandparent and grandchild, can be present even when there is no language problem – when families split, for example, and that's something mentioned briefly in Chapters 17 and 18.

What happens when your child lives abroad, and your grandchildren are brought up in a different culture, which uses a different language? If both parents speak English, there's little problem, since even if the grandchildren attend a local school, they'll use English at home, and will be bilingual into the bargain. Even if just one parent is English, there's still a good chance they'll learn and use both languages, especially if it's the mother who's the

English speaker. But even if there's no difficulty in communicating with the grandchildren, you might think of learning the local language; it won't do you any harm, and you'll get brownie points for trying. Your grandchildren will help you, of course.

Those of us who are not in direct contact with our grandchildren must prepare to enjoy the great delight of communicating with them at a distance, communicating with them as individuals in their own right.

One grandparent wrote:

> "The phone calls and letters from my grandchildren are better than any others I get. They give me a thrill every time. There's something very special about my relationship with the grandchildren, and it's wonderful to share what they're thinking and doing, and seeing it change as they grow."

So, to summarise:

- Ring your grandchildren personally, and not just when you speak to their parents.

- Prepare topics for a phone conversation.

- With young grandchildren, ask closed questions.

- Find out from the parents a good time to ring.

- Send cards frequently.

- Get used to e-mail and texting.

- If your grandchildren live abroad, think of learning the language.

CHAPTER 16

On Holiday

**"And young and old come forth to play
On a sunshine holiday."**

"Look at that family over there!" You look, and there's the typical British family on the beach, playing cricket; Joshua batting, Dad bowling, Grandpa keeping wicket, Grandma, Mum and Joshua's sister fielding. "Nice to see a real family having holiday fun," you say, taking in the three generations playing together.

Actually, three generations of a family holidaying together is not all that common a sight. What grandparents in their sixties want from a holiday is usually quite different from what parents in their forties want and, once the grandchildren are beyond the baby stage, different from what the grandchildren want. It's not easy to find a holiday that suits everyone. But it is possible: I recall a family reunion at a beach resort, where over 20 of us had a holiday together. At different times, the grandchildren surfed and played in the waves, the mothers and grandmothers explored the town, the fathers and grandfathers played bowls, and now and then everyone willing was conscripted into a game of touch rugby on the beach. It worked well for a week, but a longer period might have led to tensions!

You're likely to be asked to join the family for a holiday at sometime in your career as a grandparent: what points should you consider?

Staying with the Family

The first invitation is usually to stay with the family.

"Come and have a week with us, Grandma; it'll do you good, and Joshua would love to see you."

It's hard to refuse: especially when Joshua is an infant, and you know there'll be lots of time for bonding. Of course you won't want to sit back leisurely in a busy household; you'll want to help as well, perhaps offering to do some ironing, or take Joshua to the park, to give the parents a break. And you'll be pleased to babysit, so that the parents can have an evening out.

If you live a little way from the grandchildren, and don't see them very often, you'll probably feel that as well as seeing as much as possible of little Joshua, you'll want to help, too, if only to make up for those weeks and months when the parents have been busy coping on their own. Perhaps you weren't able to help when the grandchild was born, a time when grandmothers, in particular, usually want to help their daughters. (Even though, as mentioned earlier, some new mothers don't want grandparents around when grandchild arrives.) Fine: but do remember this isn't your own household, and the new parents probably do things differently from you. And of course, you'll be especially tactful with daughters-in-law.

The week goes well, and you enjoy it, which is the reason why so many grandparents voted 'holidays with the grandchildren' as one of their most pleasurable experiences.

But there is another sort of experience. One grandmother, with three grandchildren in New Zealand and another three in Australia, said this about her holidays with them:

"Nothing is more irritating than returning from visiting the grandchildren and having a friend say 'You're so lucky being able to have holidays in such exciting places.' I say 'Holiday! You must be joking. I've never worked so hard in my life.' After I've had a so-called holiday with my three grandchildren I need a real holiday."

And this is one reason why a few grandparents also voted holidays with the grandchildren as an activity that needs a lot of skill. But don't come away, like the grandmother above, feeling you haven't had a holiday.

By all means accept invitations to have a break with the grandchildren. When the moment is ripe, ask whether there are any local facilities for your own interests: is there a bridge club that you could visit one evening? a bowls club that would welcome visitors for an afternoon's bowls? a fishing lake for a couple of hours' sport? By all means spend nearly all the visit with the family and the grandchildren, but plan on having a little time when you can be yourself, and not merely a grandparent who's staying and being a help.

Going Away with the Family

A different holiday offer comes when the family thinks it would be nice to suggest grandparents join them on a joint holiday. The parents bait the offer: "It will be nice for Joshua and you to see more of each other."

You point out, as if they hadn't thought of it, "and you might like to have a bit of a break from being with children all day and night. You might like to have one of those evenings out together, like you used to have before the children came along."

After all, you're tame babysitters on tap, babysitters who know Joshua well – unpaid ones too. Why, they're on holiday, no work, they might be able to manage a whole day – or even two – away together, just on their own. And you'd like looking after Joshua yourself.

Why not accept the offer? It seems a good arrangement. A family holiday again after all those years will be fun. And Joshua is young, and will be happy playing on the beach with you. Even looking after him all day while the parents go off together to the local shopping centre, or cricket ground, or night club – that's fine for a day or even two. You managed your own children; there'll be no difficulty with Joshua. So you say "Yes", and you're quite prepared for the parents to have their night away, if that's what they want.

Be sure you've got a contact arrangement. All sorts of events might mean that you have to get in touch with the parents. At the very least, Joshua might suddenly feel he needs Mum and no one else; not even his favourite Gran and Grandpa will do. Perhaps talking to Mum over the phone will reassure him; but perhaps not. The important thing is that you have a contact so that the parents can decide whether to return or not.

Worse events can happen. There was the 18 month old child who climbed out of her bedroom window in the holiday flat and decided to explore the public park opposite. The first the grandparents knew of it was a police van loudhailing the neighbourhood asking whether anyone had lost a child. Not us, thought the grandparents, believing little Ruthie was fast asleep. As the van made a second circuit they thought they just ought to check. There was the empty cot…

Always have a contact number: you never know when you may need it.

Taking Grandchildren Away on Holiday

If you're taking Joshua away, it's essential to find out the sort of holiday Joshua will enjoy. You might have had lovely holidays at that hotel in Cricklade, or wherever, but Joshua may not be impressed by the chef's wonderful salmon en croute. He's far more likely to ask why they don't serve chicken nuggets, or why isn't there a swimming pool.

Planning the holiday with Joshua is fun in itself. And when you've found out the sort of holiday that he'd like, try to provide it. If Joshua has always wanted to go-kart, look for a place with a go-kart track. If Ruthie loves swimming, make sure there's a pool suitable for her age. Best of all, find a holiday place where there are likely to be other children about. That way you'll all be happy. The rule is to choose a holiday for the grandchild, not yourself.

Some grandparents suggest having a short trial run, a sort of pilot holiday, just one or possibly two nights away first. This gives you the chance of finding out how you get on together before booking, say, a week's holiday with Joshua.

Oh – one last tip: try to be around when Mum helps Joshua pack. You won't want to hear: "I can't clean my teeth; I haven't brought my toothbrush, Gran."

"Oh yes you have, Joshua. I saw it go in your case. Have another look."

And if you're a belt and braces person, as well as a contact number for the parents, you might want them to leave a statement giving you their permission to handle any emergency if for any reason they can't be contacted while you're away. Most unlikely to be needed, but you never know, and if either you or the parents are abroad, it could be important.

Going away with a grandchild on your own gives both of you an experience to cherish, one that your grandchild will remember all their life.

Looking after Teenagers

Looking after teenagers is a different matter. Most teenagers don't want to go away with you: most don't want to be looked after at all. Of course they expect you to provide their favourite meals and clean clothes, but not much else. They'll just want to socialise with their friends and listen to their favourite album. Some well-brought-up teenagers may be quite thoughtful about your own welfare. It's very pleasant to be asked if you'd like any shopping to be fetched, or a little help with the garden – but don't expect it. You're more likely to be faced with Joshua bringing in a couple of friends for a riotous jam session in the bedroom. Or more worryingly with Joshua not coming in at all.

"Where's Joshua?" you ask one of his sisters.

"Oh he's probably gone over to Dave's," or "Oh he sometimes goes to the youth club."

Either of these is said with that look that does nothing but reinforce your suspicion that the little devil's probably down at the local gambling den, or knocking back the hard stuff at the Bat and Snipe. So be sure to find out from the parents any family rules about visiting and having visitors before they leave you in charge.

All this may sound as if holidays with the grandchildren pose problems. Let's reinforce what we said earlier. Holidays with the grandchildren were actually one of the experiences that gave grandmothers and grandfathers alike great pleasure.

So, to summarise:

- A holiday with your grandchildren is fun, but:

- Do pull your weight.

- Don't be a drudge: it's your holiday too.

- If you're in sole charge, have a contact arrangement with the parents.

- Plan a holiday that suits your grandchild, not yourself.

- Supervise the bag packing.

- With teenage grandchildren, insist they follow the family rules over staying out and having friends in.

CHAPTER 17

Grandparenting when Families Crumble

Widower grandfather to five year old granddaughter.
"You're going to have a new grandmother, Jeanie."
"But I liked my old one, Gramps."
"Yes, I know, but Grannie died, and I'm going to marry Elsie."
"Why, Gramps?"
"Because I love her."
Pause: "Oh that's all right then. But don't do it again."

The little story relates to the death of a grandparent and arrival of a step-grandmother, one of many possible family changes that affect both grandparents and grandchildren. Other family changes, such as the break up of a marriage, can also have profound effects on your relationship with your grandchildren, which can change in a variety of ways. And at a time when so many marriages break up, it's not surprising that changed relationships between grandchildren and grandparents are so prevalent. Death, divorce, separation – or other events – alter all the relationships in a child's family, and grandparents are among those who are closely involved. Whether the changes are amicable or not, they do have significant effects on the children, and grandparents themselves are also going to be emotionally affected in different ways.

Loss of a Grandparent

The death of a loved grandparent can affect a child hugely, often much more than we realise. Not only are the partner and children bereaved, so are the grandchildren, for whom this may well be the first bereavement they have ever suffered. I well remember a five year old grandchild coming to me after my wife died and asking sadly: "Why did Grannie have to die, Grandad?"

That's a question exposing the whole human situation. How you answer it depends so much on your own personal philosophy, whether rationalist or religious or whatever. What is essential is that we realise how much children can be upset by the death of a grandparent, and that they may not find it as easy as my little five year old did to express their worries.

Some, who find it hard to talk about this new experience, may find it easier to write about their loss. When I asked children to write down something about their grandparents, I was surprised how prominently death was in their thoughts, and so was mentioned in many of the stories they wrote.

"The hospital killed my Grandad. He died when they cut an artery or a vein."

Or just: "My Mum's Mum died the winter that I was born."

It's always helpful if someone in the family, at an appropriate moment, gently opens up how the grandchild feels about the death of a loved grandparent. Call it counselling, or call it sympathetic humanity, sharing a feeling of loss does help a child, who may not know how to handle a new and potentially troubling experience.

New Grandparents

Another aspect to rearranged relationships is the arrival of a new person in the grandparent role, whether legally a step-grandparent or not. Of course this can be helpful and positive; not always, however. Here's a 10 year old writing about her grandparents:

"My Grandma lives in Spain. She tells me funny stories. I see her once a year. When she moved to Spain my Grandad died. He went to the war, but survived and died about three years ago, and that was my saddest story until my Grandma got married to my step-Grandad. He doesn't like me much and always makes a fuss..."

What can be done about relationships between a new partner and your grandchildren? It's easy to say 'your new partner ought to be (nearly) as fond of your grandchildren as you are', but so many other considerations affect the relationships we make. In an ideal world a new step-grandparent would indeed be as fond of your grandchildren as you are yourself, but the world is not ideal. Just be careful, and weigh up how much your relationships with your grandchildren mean to you before making commitments. And good luck!

Of course you may be in the position of being a step-grandparent yourself. Perhaps, through divorce, the true grandparent is still around, or perhaps through death, for example, he or she is not. Tread carefully: either way you can't be a replacement for the grandparent who's not there. To the grandchild you're a new adult in the grandparent role, and as a new adult the child will take you as you are. Those tricks you play with your own grandchildren will be as amusing to the step-grandchildren as to your own. Little gifts to show your fondness for them, taking part in their activities, in short being a good family member in as many ways as possible will help to cement the new relationship.

Ask the parents how you can please your new step-grandchild – what does he like doing? What does he like playing? Ask him, too: what football team does he follow? and so on. In short show interest in him and his activities. But don't rush it; let little Hughie take his time in getting to know you – going slowly is better than hurrying. In a phrase, be your natural tactful self.

There are so many different grandparent-grandchildren relationships possible. One couple I know had a child, Edward, who had the conventional set of four grandparents. His parents divorced and each remarried, each new spouse having two parents. This brought Edward four new 'grandparents'. One of the second marriages foundered, and Edward's mother remarried for the second time, bringing him two more grandparent figures, giving Edward 10 in all. When the parental relationships change so drastically, a sympathetic grandparent, still playing a steady grandparent role, can offer a welcome security in a child's world that's changing so dramatically

When Parents Break Up

What happens to the grandparent role when the parents break up? Many would expect the grandparents to play a much bigger part in the life of the grandchildren. In fact this is only partly true. Broadly speaking, surveys show that those grandparents who are not heavily involved with the grandchildren before the break up, remain quite distant after the break up. On the other hand, those grandparents who are deeply interested in their grandchildren beforehand, become even more committed afterwards.

As an example of the first situation one mother wrote:

> "My own father and in-laws are unable or unwilling to be involved any more than superficially in my children's lives. It is very hurtful. They [the children] are truly missing having someone who they can relate to with love, and who is not strictly in the parental role. I am currently trying to find foster grandparents for them."

Here is the opposite example, showing that support can also come from the grandparents whose child doesn't have custody of the grandchildren. This mother wrote:

"My ex-husband left me with three children aged 10, eight, and five; the five year old had Down's syndrome. Although shattered by his actions, my parents-in-law made a positive decision to give their grandchildren as much care and support as they could, particularly my Down's daughter. This of course helped me considerably."

The foster grandparent solution mentioned by the first mother has been formalised in the USA where older adults, willing to act as a foster grandparent to a child, can, in some cases, apply for a government grant in return. It is a recognition that in a hard pressed family, children can benefit from the presence of an older adult who is willing to cook a meal for them, take them out to special events, do all the kind of things that real grandparents do.

Remember that divorce, like bereavement, is as much of a blow to the grandchildren as to the parents, and perhaps more so. Some of your grandchildren might be troubled by complicated feelings of guilt – "Was it because of me that Mummy and Daddy quarrelled?" So as well as possibly needing extra care at a difficult time, they also need someone to talk to. If you feel you can fulfil that role, good. If not, discuss with the parents the possibility of involving a neutral figure like a counsellor or educational psychologist. Often the school can help – and of course the school ought to be advised of the change in the family situation, if only to make allowances for any consequent changes in the grandchildren's behaviour and performance. If the school is not aware of the change, any troublesome behaviour or poor work might result in punishment, rather than understanding and help.

Some grandparents are very heavily involved with their grandchildren when families crumble. In some situations grandparents feel they have to assume the whole responsibility for rearing the children, particularly when the alternative is letting the children be taken into care. This is a tremendous responsibility at a time of life when energy is lower, when income is reduced, and when there may be members of the older generation needing care themselves. Having fun with the grandchildren when they go home at the end of the day is one thing: bringing them up is another.

Bringing up Grandchild

Bringing up grandchild is actually a very old tradition. In some close knit communities, for example the South Wales mining valleys of the nineteenth century, it was sometimes the custom for the first child of a marriage to be brought up by the grandmother. It was a practice that gave the grandmother a purpose when her own children had grown up, and it relieved the young mother at a time when she was becoming adjusted to her new role as wife. It also helped her learn the skill of bringing up children by observing and helping an experienced mother. Of course mother and grandmother lived near each other, perhaps in the next street or even in the same house, so mother and child were still very close.

That was an arrangement of choice, not of necessity. Today, some grandparents are forced into bringing up grandchild by circumstances beyond their control. How many grandparents are bringing up their grandchildren?

A recent study by Frank Field, the former government minister, estimated that there are some 130,000 'pensioner parents', effectively fostering their grandchildren in place of troubled or absent mothers and fathers. These 130,000 are scattered across the country, and in many cases their unusual situation causes a variety of concerns.

The cost of raising the grandchild is one of these grandparents' main worries. Bringing up children is a costly experience, a truth that is brought sharply home when you start again late in life.

Some grandparents postpone retirement; some who have already retired feel the need to return to work to meet the costs involved; some dip heavily into their own savings; others rely on the social services for support. If you've made a permanent arrangement to bring up your grandchild you're entitled to claim Family Allowance, but those seeking support from the social services did complain about the complexity of the different benefits from which they might be able to get some support.

Don't think that you won't get support because you aren't the parent. There are various routes to assistance that you're entitled to have. Get advice from your local Citizen's Advice Bureau; contact one of the organisations for grandparents – for example The Grandparents Association, (see the Acknowledgements); seek out others in the same situation and talk things over.

Another issue that concerns grandparents in this situation is their own ageing. In all those little jobs like taking the children to school, you'll be very conscious of the generation difference between yourself and the other parents (as too will the grandchild). These grandparents wonder whether they will keep well enough to finish the task of rearing the grandchild, or whether their advancing years will mean eventually having to hand the child's care to someone else. Some of these pensioner parents take on this new responsibility at a time in their lives when they also have to look after their own frail and deteriorating parents – unsung heroes indeed.

It's right to think carefully before taking on such a huge responsibility. Little three year olds who look so sweet and so appealing, tugging at heartstrings, in a dozen years time will become large, demanding adolescents. You will be 12 years older then, an inescapable change you must bear in mind.

Yes, there are pressures, but these make it more than ever necessary to keep a bit of time for your own life. Keep contact with the groups and societies for your own age group. If need be, and if it's appropriate, take the grandchild along. In other words, don't isolate yourself.

So, to summarise:

- Don't avoid discussing the death of a family member…

- …but do handle it sensitively.

- Don't expect a grandchild immediately to love a new grandparent as you might hope.

- Build the relationship slowly and carefully.

- If the parents break up, a grandchild may need help to understand the situation, and if so, try to find a sympathetic person, skilled at talking things over with children.

- Ensure that someone, probably a parent, makes the school aware of changes in the grandchild's home circumstances, if schoolwork deteriorates.

- Don't rush to offer to raise your grandchild yourself when the parents split up. Consider the implications carefully: it may not be the best solution in any case.

If you do raise your grandchild yourself:

- Do make full use of the financial support available.

- Don't isolate yourself; stay a member of your various societies and join a grandparents' organisation.

- Remember that raising a grandchild yourself can create a great bond of love between you and the grandchild you raise.

CHAPTER 18

Grandparents' Rights

"All's love, yet all's law."

This book has emphasised grandparents' relationships with their grandchildren. These relationships are usually straightforward and happy, with both you and your grandchild looking forward to seeing each other whenever it suits you and the family. But this state of affairs doesn't always exist. What happens when obstacles are put in your way, when strong feelings on the part of others try to prevent you seeing your grandchild? Are you entitled to have access to your grandchild? What are your rights?

Contact Orders

After parents go their own separate ways, the grandchild, either through mutual consent or by a court order, usually lives with one or other of them. You, the grandparent, naturally want to retain, and perhaps strengthen that bond that exists between you and your little Charlotte. Hopefully, the parent with whom the grandchild lives will allow and perhaps encourage that relationship.

But sadly there are many situations where the break up has been bitter and rancorous. The parent who believes he or she has been 'wronged' may be bringing up your little Charlotte. If that parent is your son or daughter, then there is usually little difficulty in continuing to see her. In fact, you may well be asked for an even greater degree of support than previously.

If that parent is your daughter-in-law, or son-in-law, the situation changes. Perhaps, as was illustrated in one of the earlier comments from a mother, your interest and support will be welcome. But it might not be. And in some situations the parent in charge may deliberately refuse to allow you, the grandparent, to see little Charlotte. Perhaps revenge plays a part in this. Or perhaps the parent genuinely feels that regular visits with grandparent may disturb the family equilibrium. You can't bear the thought of losing all contact with Charlotte. Do you, as the grandparent, have a right of access to your grandchild?

Unfortunately, no. In many countries, and in many if not all States in the USA, grandparents do have such rights. But in England and Wales those rights were abolished some years ago. Nowadays you, the grandparent, have to seek leave to apply for a court order to be able to see and visit little Charlotte. If leave is granted, you then apply to the court for what is called a 'contact order'. This two stage process is designed, apparently, to deter those individuals who might wish to apply for a contact order on trivial grounds, or who might wish to involve any 'opponents' in irritating and perhaps costly court proceedings for vindictive reasons. Family breakdowns can involve bitter feelings, and repeated court requests for contact orders, reopening old wounds and perhaps involving legal expenses, could be one way of seeking revenge. Hence the court will first determine whether the motive for your application is a reasonable one, and if it is, may grant you leave to apply for a contact order.

Residence Orders

Who is responsible for a grandchild who is living permanently with you, the grandparent? How can it be established that you, though not the parent, are really in full charge of the child, so that no one can remove the grandchild from your care? (It is also important to establish who is in charge of the child for all those situations where 'parental consent' is needed – school trips, to take a simple example.) There are different sorts of court orders that can give your grandchild some security; the most common is called a 'residence order'. This is a court order determining with whom a child shall live.

Applying for a residence order is not quite as straightforward as it seems. First, you have to seek the court's leave to apply for a residence order. If leave is granted, you make the application. In other words, this is a two stage process, similar to that required for the contact order mentioned above.

Of course let's hope that legal proceedings are not needed, and that any tensions between grandparents and parents can, in the interests of the grandchildren, be smoothed over without going to the courts.

What to Do if There are Difficulties

So far, this chapter has just given a short sketch of the legal position in England and Wales. Going to the courts has been mentioned more than once. But few of us want to get involved with a court if we can avoid it. The alternative, and a path well worth trying first, is mediation, in the hope that someone else may be able to reconcile the differences between you and your opponent without having to fight them out in court. For mediation you need someone to act as a mediator. Who might fill the role?

Someone who knows the family situation, but who is a neutral figure in the dispute, is a possibility. Perhaps you're friendly with a relative on 'the other side' who might be willing to try to act as a go-between in healing the rift. It's a delicate task, and not everyone would want to get involved, even though the wellbeing of a child is a considerable incentive.

Alternatively, an organisation can sometimes help. One worth consulting is the Grandparents Association (see the summary below), which supports the use of mediation. But mediation has to be acceptable to both sides in the dispute.

If mediation isn't possible, or if it's tried and failed, then you might want to use the law. Talk over the possible effect on your grandchild before taking definite steps, perhaps with others who have been in the same situation. And if you do decide that it's in your grandchild's interest to fight this battle, do find a good solicitor, well versed in family law.

So, to summarise:

- There is at present no legal right in England and Wales for grandparents to have access to their grandchild.

- Visit the Grandparents Association website **www.grandparents-association.org.uk** and review others' experiences.

- If you are unfairly prevented from seeing your grandchild, try mediation before applying to the courts.

- Apply to the courts for a residence order if your grandchild lives with you permanently.

- Get legal advice from a good solicitor well versed in family law.

CHAPTER 19

Great-grandchildren

"My great-nana is 93, but she's still very independent and still makes marmalade. She makes lunch for Nana and Pops every Friday."

It's appropriate to end with yet another new birth, the arrival of the first great-grandchild. As the first chapter stressed, grandparents today are generally fitter, and generally live longer than previously. More and more of us live to see the arrival of our great-grandchildren. Our children's children, the little ones that we've played with, helped to nurture, seen through their adolescence and helped to start on their adult lives – our grandchildren – become parents themselves.

It really does mark the passage of time and of life when you become the senior of four generations. It's a time for reflection, as well as a time for celebration. Perhaps because of age, or perhaps because of the bitter sweet element at seeing life move on, leaving us stranded in another, earlier time, the great-grandparents I know don't hold major celebrations. Of course they want to mark the arrival of the new generation, usually with a personal gift, perhaps something they've made themselves, something that the new arrival will be able to appreciate and perhaps cherish in years to come. And yes, of course they want to see the new member of the family, either by the baby being proudly brought to them, together with camera, or if still fit and well, by making the journey to see them. There'll be photographs of great-grandparents with the baby, and photographs of the four family generations, to be placed in various family albums.

But there isn't the pressing feeling that you want to help with the child, as there was with the arrival of your grandchildren. After all, there are now two generations, your children and your grand-children, all mature adults, between you and the baby. Between them, they should be able to cope, just as you coped when your grandchild arrived. This is a time to sit back and reflect, and to enjoy the news of your great-grandchild's development that you'll hear from your children and your grandchildren. Responsibilities are over.

Relax: there's no better time.

The Survey

The survey mentioned in the book, and which appears on the next two pages, was the main guide for deciding the content. After chatting with experienced grandparents, I compiled a list of 28 situations that figured prominently in their concerns, and sent it out to well over 100 grandparents. Eighty-four grandparents returned questionnaires, usually but not always fully completed. In addition the survey items were presented informally to 20 others, making a sample of just over 100 grandparents. The ratio of grandmothers to grandfathers was 2:1. Some of the interesting observations freely offered are mentioned in the book, and where the grandparents offered a phone number for contact, it gave a chance to hear their views in more detail.

You might like to compare the situations that our grandparents voted most pleasing, and those that needed skill to handle, with your own views. So I give below the results for the 10 most voted situations in each case. (Bear in mind that the grandparents surveyed ticked more than one answer, so the total number of votes adds up to a lot more than the number of grandparents surveyed.)

Situations giving most pleasure	No. of votes
Watching your grandchild develop	37
Having your grandchild to stay	33
Holding your first grandchild	29
News that a grandchild is expected	24

Playing with your grandchild	23
Holidays with your grandchild	22
Seeing all your grandchildren together	17
Getting phone calls from your grandchild	9
Getting letters/e-mails/drawings from your grandchild	8

Situations requiring most skill	**No. of votes**
Giving advice on child-rearing to the parents	38
Using your experience of child-rearing again	20
Having your grandchild to stay	19
Relationships with your grandchild after parents have parted	17
Comforting your grandchild when upset	16
Making financial arrangements for your grandchild's future	14
Being a carer for Mum to work	10
The changed relationship with your daughter-in-law	9
The relationship with the other grandparents	8
The changed relationship with your own daughter	8